FAITH REDISCOVERED

Coming Home to Catholicism

FAITH REDISCOVERED

Coming Home to Catholicism

Lawrence Cunningham

Paulist Press/New York, Mahwah

Library of Congress Cataloging-in-Publication Data

Cunningham, Lawrence.
    Faith rediscovered : coming home to Catholicism
        p.   cm.
    Bibliography: p.
    ISBN 0-8091-2923-X (pbk.)
        1. Catholic Church—Apologetic works.   2. Catholic Church—
Doctrines.   I. Title.
BX1754.C836 1987   87-20299
230'.2—dc19   CIP

Published by Paulist Press
997 Macarthur Boulevard
Mahwah, NJ 07430

Printed and bound in the
United States of America

Contents

Introduction 1

I   Leaving 3

II   Faith and the Faith 18

III   Worship 32

IV   The Catholic Church 43

V   Living as a Catholic 54

VI   Coming Back to the Church 71

VII A Catholic Invitation 84

Appendix: Some Basic Readings 96

Introduction

For the past few years there has been a concerted effort, carried out at various levels in the Church, to encourage people to return to the practice of the faith. When Pope John Paul II visited Australia in the fall of 1986 he made such a plea himself. Speaking to a huge crowd in Sydney he invited those who had left the Church to "come home again" in order, as the Pope said, to take a place amid God's people—a place "that you alone can fill."

This little book is addressed to those who have decided to come back to the practice of the faith or who are at least open to that idea. It is not so much a "how to" manual to make that return as it is an encouragement to take that step. No book can sort out the complex issues that affect a person who wants to make a faith decision, and this one does not try to do so. What it does attempt to do is to set out the basic faith of Catholics and, in the process, to insist that persons who want to return are welcome; their presence is desired; their absence has been felt.

The idea for this book came from the editors of Paulist Press. They encouraged me to write it. I would like to thank Father Kevin Lynch and Douglas Fisher of the Press for their encouragement and help. Andrew Greeley also encouraged me and supplied me with some helpful material. During the course of writing the book I spoke to a large number of people about the subject and received much guidance from them. Their names are too numerous to mention but I would like to acknowledge Walter Moore, the chair of the Religion Department at Florida State and my other colleagues in that department for making life easy enough to do one's work. Maureen Jackson initiated me into the mysteries of the word processor for which I am grateful. Finally, a word of thanks and love to my wife Cecilia and our daughters Sarah Mary and Julia Clare who always welcome me home.

I
Leaving

Here is a scenario that every college chaplain and many parents can understand: a young man or woman, beneficiaries of a close-knit Catholic family and a parochial school education, goes off to school a practicing Catholic and comes home a self-described ''ex-Catholic'' or ''non-practicing Catholic.'' When queried by anxious parents as to the reason why they are no longer interested in the Church, the answers are, by turn, evasive or non-existent. It just happens. If we were to think about the reasons ourselves, the list of possible reasons could well be immense: influential teachers who were not sympathetic to the faith; companions who led the student astray; a member of the opposite sex who was more attractive than Mass attendance; etc.

There is another plausible explanation which we would like to propose as an explanation for this defection. Let us assume that Mike, a college student, goes to Mass each Sunday at the campus chapel as it was expected of him. One Sunday, after a late party, he does not respond to the alarm clock. Waking up at noon, too late for the last Sunday liturgy, he discovers three things: (a) there was no mom or dad there to get him up and out of the door; (b) there were a fair number of others who also did not get up for Sunday worship; (c) he does not feel all that guilty. Let us further assume that under the pressure of study or through the discovery of what one could do on a Sunday morning, the custom of going to Mass soon turns into an occasional event. To explain or rationalize this change of life style, Mike begins to say (first to himself and then, in time, to others) that he did not ''get much'' out of church. The conclusion he finally comes to is that he has ''lost his faith.''

Is that, in fact, what has happened? It may well be that after a period of neglect such people will cut all ties with the church of their youth, in fact. It may also be that, in time, they will come back to the practice of their faith. In either case we can still raise the question as to whether they did "lose their faith."

My inclination is to answer that question in the negative. What seems more plausible to me is that what they have lost is a certain pattern of behavior, reinforced by family, neighborhood, school, and church, about which they have never given much thought in a deeply personal way. What has happened, basically, is that they have put off something that was expected of them as youths but which now does not fit into the way they live or want to live. Chances are that when they are at home on vacation they will go back to church with their family since that is a family thing to do and their parents expect it.

We have used the example of the college student but it does not take a great effort to see that the same thing can easily happen as one goes off to the military, or marries, or moves to a new town for a new job. In short, some people leave the Church, not through some dramatic crisis, but because they feel that they have out-grown a certain kind of learned behavior which was typical of a certain stage in life. The practice of the faith is something that is left behind like scouting or collecting baseball cards: it just does not seem to fit in anymore.

Of course, not everyone leaves the Church through this rather easy drifting away that comes with adulthood. Some people leave the Church through a wrenchingly bad experience or through a real crisis of belief that can be, but is not always, traumatic. Who has not heard of people who have had a terrible personal crisis that involves the Church at some level? It may be something as simple as an unkind cleric or religious (how many people have soured on the Church because of the cruelty of a parochial school teacher?) or as shattering as the experience of a friend of mine whose father was denied Christian burial by an overbearing pastor because suicide was suspected in the man's death.

A crisis of belief can come either as a sort of counter-revelation or through some profound trauma. Michael Harrington, the noted social philosopher, recounts in his autobiographical memoir *Fragments of a Century* how, as a passionately devoted Catholic Worker he went off on a bus trip to speak at a certain parish. As he stepped off the bus, he suddenly said to himself that he no longer believed what he believed when he got on the bus just a few hours before. With that sense of suddenness he became a kind of Catholic outsider, profoundly sympathetic to the Church and what it teaches, but no longer able to say the creeds of his religion. His case is hardly unique. Our libraries are full of books by thinkers who acknowledge their debt to the Catholic tradition but who simply no longer find it possible to believe; thus, George Santayana, the Harvard philosopher, once described himself as a "Catholic atheist."

By far, the most common reason why people become estranged from the Church is because they find a tension, seen as unresolvable, between what they think they must or must not do and what the Church seemingly demands of them. Such tensions loom as a stark either/or, and in deciding against the Church they find themselves, despite deep roots in the Church, estranged from a Church which they seemingly love. Examples of this kind of estrangement are to be found in every neighborhood and in most Catholic families in this country and around the world: people see no alternative to birth control; for many and varied reasons people procure abortions; people marry someone with different or no faith convictions; people are gay or remarried outside the Church. The examples of this kind can be multiplied in any number of permutations.

Recent changes in the Catholic Church have also precipitated seemingly unresolvable tensions which bear, not on moral behavior, but on the very manner in which the Catholic faith is experienced. Such tensions appear on both the right and the left side of the religious spectrum. Many conservatives feel "left out" of a Church which they once knew and loved. They complain that a sense of mystery and solidity and discipline has been traded for a modernist mess of pottage. That this is a real problem is evidenced by such breakaway movements as the Catholic Traditionalists who, in some of their manifestations, have become a schismatic movement. Not a few people have left Roman Catholicism for the seemingly immobile assurances of Eastern Orthodoxy. Others, less adventuresome in their moves, simply stand at the sidelines, shaking their heads at the passing of a Catholic tradition that they once loved but now seems dead. As a friend of mine once remarked: "When the Church lost Latin, they also lost me."

It is clear that not everyone has left the Catholic Church because the pace of change since the Second Vatican Council has been too fast and too dramatic. Many people, first exhilarated by the rapid changes in the Church, soon became discouraged that the pace of change did not keep up with their expectations. Father Andrew Greeley, for example, has argued rather persuasively that the 1968 encyclical *Humane Vitae* which reaffirmed the traditional Catholic opposition to contraception was almost single-handedly responsible for the sharp falloff in Catholic practice in the late 1960s and 1970s. Many married couples were convinced that the ban on contraception would be lifted or drastically modified. When that did not happen, they saw looming obstacles in their desire to remain faithful Catholics and, in many instances, "voted with their feet."

Another issue now presents itself to those who desire change in the Church: the feminist issue. The rise of the feminist movement has had a profound impact on the social life of this country, as is clear from the daily reading of the newspapers. Even those who reject the tag of "feminist" have absorbed the prevailing sense that women are no longer willing or able to remain subservient to men as second class citizens. Women have entered the work force on a level of parity, made inroads in the professions, and have won legal and social acceptance in a manner that was unthinkable a generation ago. It was inevitable that such a revolution (and make no mistake about it—there has been a revolution) would also challenge the innate conservatism of the Church. It may be true that only a few activist persons will spend energies to struggle for the right of women's ordination to the priesthood, but it is clear that deeply rooted prejudices against women have so "turned off" many well educated women that they have simply quietly (and not so quietly) left the Church as an oppressive and uncaring institution that gives them no place within it.

Careful readers of the above paragraphs will note that we have spoken mainly of leaving the Church rather than "losing the faith." The two issues are, and must be, separated. In the next section we will specify that distinction a bit more clearly. For now, we want to emphasize the situation of those who, for various reasons, leave the boundaries of the Church at least in the sense that their connection with the Church is either non-existent or very tenuous. This "cutting of the ties" most often gets articulated by phrases like those oft-repeated words: "I am a Catholic but not a very good one," or "I am a Catholic but do not practice my faith."

An analogy might be helpful here. It is a well-known fact that many people who were safely in the traditional Democratic camp in this country have now abandoned the Democratic Party to become either Republicans or Independents. That shift, say, of the typical working class ethnic voter in the northeast may argue that he or she has not left the party; the party has left them. Others, from another perspective, might argue that the Democrats are so anxious to ape the policies of the Republicans that they feel they must defect and become Independents. In either case, these wandering Democrats would be quick to assert that they have never

left the ideals of the party: justice for the working person; social
concern for the needy; etc. It just is, these defectors will say, that
these things don't seem to happen in the party to which they first
gave their allegiance and support. The democratic ideals are still
there but the party has either shifted or finds no room for them.
That is a situation which, I suspect, many people find in the Catholic Church of today.

What is the attitude of those who have left? To that question,
obviously, no simple answer can be given. There may be great
and enduring bitterness accompanied by total rejection of the
Church. For others there may be deep sense of guilt born of an
early education that insisted that to reject the Church was to reject
the ordinary means of eternal salvation. Still others may feel a tremendous nostalgia for the simple faith of their youth in tandem
with a conviction that there is no going home again. Still another
group may simply be biding their time; they are not practicing but
they feel that someday they would like to return. And, finally,
there are those who would like to come back home but are either
fearful or uncertain or bewildered as to how to accomplish that
return.

This book addresses itself to those who have been away from
the Church but who feel some inclination to return. It does not
pretend that it can answer all of the questions about that return.
What it does hope to do is to offer a word of encouragement and
a reflection on the process of returning.

We should begin by noting that many in the Church are aware
of the many who have left. There are organized campaigns, ad-
vertising programs, and formal movements to encourage people
to come back to the Church. Many dioceses use everything from
highway billboards to television spots to say to people that they
are missed and that they would find a welcome should they decide
to come back to the Church.

Implicit in that campaign are two very basic and extremely important assumptions: that the Church extends a hand and that the

Church itself may bear some responsibility either directly or in-directly for the alienation of some people. The open invitation to come home should not be viewed as the superior gesture of some overly righteous parent who welcomes back a prodigal; it should be more likened to a person who misses a loved one who is absent through a mutual falling out.

Many people have the feeling that the Church sees itself as "perfect" and those who disagree with it as somehow "obsti-nate" or "faithless." The plain fact of the matter is, however, that the Church is an imperfect instrument precisely because it is noth-ing more than the people of God who are imperfect. To see the condition of the Church one need not do more than look around at any local congregation on any Sunday. That is the Church. The hypothetical congregation that one views will have some extraor-dinary people in it and some others who are mediocre and a few who are unworthy of the name Christian. After all, Jesus in the Gospels compares the Church to a field which has both wheat and weeds. It is only in the final days that the perfect and imperfect can be separated.

We should not confuse the reality of the Church with its visible leadership. Those who represent the hierarchy might be inclined to put the "best face" on the Church and/or insist on its divine order and its godly powers, but even the most loyal hierarch un-derstands that the Church is an institution that reflects the fragility of the human condition. That fact becomes abundantly clear when, for instance, we look at the documents issued by the world's bishops at the Second Vatican Council. The fathers at that council insisted on taking a hard look at the Church in all of its accomplishments and in all of its deficiencies. While it set out a picture of the Church as it would like it to be, it also took the ex-traordinary step of admitting that it also had to accept blame for part of the deficiencies of religious life. Thus, in the *Decree on Ecumenism* (I.4) the council not only admitted its deficiencies as a Church but insisted on the need to correct those things which prevent the Church from being an effective instrument of the Gospel of Jesus Christ.

WHY RETURN?

We have offered a number of reasons to explain why a person might leave the Church. We have also insisted that the Church invites those who have left, and who want to return, to come back to the Church. We might further our preliminary explorations here by asking why a person might consider returning to the practice of the faith. That is a very large question and admits to as many answers as the question of why people leave in the first place.

For some people it is as simple as the sentiment behind the phrase "coming home." For many people being a Catholic is so much a part of who they are that it would be unthinkable of them to define themselves without reference to their family faith. I remember a friend of mine who, leaving his deep south home for college in the northeast, left his ancestral faith to join the Episcopal Church. When he went back home to teach he eventually enrolled as a member of a local Baptist congregation. He said that what he learned as he went home to teach was that he was, pure and simple, a Baptist. "That," he said to me emphatically, "is who I am." Anyone who was raised in a strong Catholic family will understand the sentiment behind that assertion.

That sense of "who I am" is often coupled with a desire to establish some sense of structure in one's personal life and, by extension, in family life. The students who have drifted away from the practice of their religion that we mentioned at the start of this chapter will often resume the practice of their faith as they depart from college and begin to make their way in the world. It is part of the process of growing up. There is a bit of a paradox here: just as people leave the Church because they identify it with their childhood, so they often return to it as a sign of their maturity.

Connected to that sense of "who I am" is something that is more than nostalgia but akin to longing for a sense of the Sacred associated with the best moments of Catholic faith. Saint Paul once wrote that faith is from hearing, but for me faith comes, or, better, is reinforced, by smelling. My best memories of my Catholic experience come when, for instance, I go to Midnight Mass on Christmas Eve and that peculiar blend of incense, evergreen fragrance, beeswax, new clothing, and the crisp air of the season floods my memory of Christmases past. That triggered memory is not pure sentimentality. It is, rather, an assurance that certain things endure, that a certain continuity exists in life, and that, within the Church, there are seasons, occasions, and events that mark off the intrusion of grace into one's life. I, then, celebrate the birth of Christ just as my parents, and theirs before them, celebrated. It is part of my history.

For still others, a return to the faith comes not from the gentle tug of the past but because of the crises or pressures of the present. In other words, some people return to the Church because they have a real and urgent need for the Church. This involves more than nostalgia; it may occur either from some genuine moment of enlightenment or from a certain imminent or real crisis either personal or social.

By enlightenment I do not mean the proverbial lightbulb going on over one's head. What I have in mind, rather, is that time in one's life when it becomes very clear that everything is either not as it should be or that things seem to be headed in the wrong direction. This moment happens, not infrequently, when a young couple, with a child or two approaching school age, begin to understand that something is required, beyond their family bonds, to give them the strength and the sustenance to be a genuine family. This "enlightenment" may come at a time when both parents realize that they are so busy doing things, making a living, and getting by that there is either very little time or inclination to focus their energies as a family. This is often a time when people say that they ought go back to church or "join a church" in order to find encouragement for the very real problems that militate against family stability and family harmony.

At a more urgent level, some people sense either a lack in their life or a feeling that things have just gotten out of control. To use the words of W. B. Yeats their "centre does not hold." Either because of general dissatisfaction or some real and describable void in their lives, people will reach out for something larger and more solid within which they can frame their lives into some meaningful whole. They want to find something "more" which seems beyond the grasp of their own efforts.

That something "more" becomes all the greater when a person's life is touched by tragedy. Many years ago I met a woman who found her way back to the Church after the brutal kidnaping and murder of her young son. She told me that she came to church to pray out of a sense of absolute desolation that nothing could sustain her through the agony of her experience. "It was either God or suicide," she said to me one day. Her experience was terrible but not unique.

If faith does nothing else, it gives to people a vocabulary and a set of promises that the absurd tragedies of life are not, in any ultimate sense, meaningless or beyond bearing. It is precisely at those moments, it seems to me, that the Church can most surely move into a person's life. That is not to say that the Church can provide easy answers or quick slogans to heal pain and agony. What the Church can do is stand in solidarity with the pained person or family and say, by its witness, that their suffering is not theirs alone and not meaningless.

We all know those sort of cultural Catholics who turn to the Church only on the rarest of occasions. They may go to Mass at Christmas and Easter, they probably have their children baptized, they want to marry in the Church (but would not hesitate much to do otherwise), and, having seen the priest on their deathbed, would certainly want him present at their funeral. This kind of Catholic is the subject of much concern to those who are active in the Church. However, this much ought be said in their defense: there is more than ingrained habit in their way of looking at the Church. There may well be a kind of habitual reflex but one could also argue that their very actions demonstrate that, almost instinctively, they recognize that it is to the Church they should turn at those critical moments of a person's life—the times of birth, maturity, sickness, and death. That, obviously, is not all there is to the practice of the faith, but it is a start and not a false one at that.

There is another point. If a person comes to church infrequently and/or only for special moments, that person is paying tribute to a very deep insight with respect to religious practice. Religion, in the final analysis, deals with those issues and questions which touch the deepest strands of human existence: Who am I? What does my life mean for me and others? What direction is my life taking? What, ultimately, is to happen to me? Only the philosophically inclined ponder those questions with persistence or in a systematic manner. But everyone, at a given moment in life, faces those questions in the context of living. It is at that moment, or, in those moments, that the need for religion becomes clear and compelling.

Religion, in that sense, gives a center to one's living. By the practice of faith one affirms that there is something beyond and around and under (all the words are pertinent) our own limited life. When we worship together, for instance, we are saying a number of things by the very act of worship. We affirm the reality of God and the primacy of Jesus Christ in our lives; we affirm a comradeship with the community of believers; we affirm our need to listen to God's word and to live out its meaning. Overarching all of those affirmations is the deeper affirmation that we are not left alone, we are not fully autonomous; rather, we are a people who can cry out in faith: "Our Father."

RETURNING

Later in this book we will deal with some of the practical issues about returning to the practice of the faith. At this juncture we wish only to offer a few words of encouragement to those who would like to return to the faith but feel that there are difficulties in making the return. While working on this chapter I spoke to a number of people, both those who are "professionals" in the Church (priests, sisters, pastoral workers, etc.) and lay folks either practicing or not practicing their faith. My queries (I would not like to claim that it was research in any meaningful sense of the term) have led me to believe that there are a number of hesitations and/or problems confronting those who would like to return to the faith. In the course of this book we will treat some of the issues raised by these questions. At this point we should merely take note of them if for no other reason than to alert the reader that we are aware of these issues. In no order of importance, let me mention some of the things I have heard:

(1) *There are still many things which the Church teaches with which I disagree.* About this objection two things can be said very briefly. The first is that one must distinguish between what one might believe the Church teaches and the actual teaching of the Church. Many people go through life with a head full of misinformation gathered together from half understood lessons from their catechism days and popular glosses on that misinformation. A rather well informed executive told me that he just did not believe that he was going to hell for eating meat on Fridays as "the nuns told him"—that sort of thing. One step, then, is to get informed and precise knowledge about what the Church, in fact, does and does not teach.

Secondly, we should insist that faith is not a total and complete submission to everything that is part of the Church's teaching. As the Second Vatican Council said, there is a hierarchy of truth in Christianity. We need to affirm in faith those things which are central to the faith or, to phrase it somewhat differently, we need to celebrate Jesus Christ within the community of faith and in that faith we grow to a deeper and more faith-filled appreciation of how the Church sustains that central affirmation of the Gospel. Faith is not, for most of us, a blinding once-in-a-lifetime experience of conversion. It is, rather, an incremental growth from a deep basic trust by which, through a series of conversions, we conform ourselves to the will of God as we learn it. Hence, our prayer should be the prayer of the Gospel: "I believe, Lord. Help my unbelief."

(2) *There are certain aspects of my life which are not in harmony with Church policy.* This is a very common fear or self-imposed obstacle. One hears it in various forms: "I'm 'out of the Church' because I am married to a divorced person" or because "I wasn't married in the Church" or because "I practice birth control" or "I've had an abortion and am excommunicated."

We should begin by saying that traditionally the Church has taught that there is no unforgivable sin beyond the sin of despair (which is a refusal to believe that one can be forgiven) and, secondly, that Christ teaches mercy and forgiveness, not exclusion and ostracism. At this point, without discussing the details of specific cases, let it be said simply that there is no impossible situation. Even before "talking to a priest" (the usual advice) one should simply go back to church and enter into the prayer life of the liturgy. It is within the context of the life of prayer that problems should be located and, ultimately, solved.

(3) *I feel great guilt with respect to things in my life.* The word *remorse* comes from two Latin words *re* and *mordere* which mean, literally, "to bite again and again." At times things have happened in our lives that we cannot seem to get over. We brood about unkindnesses we have uttered that have hurt people; we regret our past acts of malice or weakness. Sometimes people become haunted by such acts and their situation is made worse by a strong sense of guilt fostered by early religious upbringing. We

should be frank enough as Catholics to admit that the Church has been a powerful instrument for fostering guilt. Be that as it may, we should also realize one powerful and basic fact: we can be forgiven and the source of forgiveness is one of the primary ministries of the Church. The Catholic Church has never claimed to be a perfectionist sect which admits only the sainted perfect. We are a sinful people who ask God's forgiveness every time we gather to worship. Furthermore, one of the sacraments of the Church is the sacrament of penance or, as it is often called today, the sacrament of reconciliation. It is within the Church that we can be reconciled with the Church as a community, and, most importantly, with God who is the source of forgiveness.

(4) *I still feel some bitterness toward the Church.* Many people who wish to return to the practice of the faith have a kind of double attitude toward that return. On the one hand, they feel a need to be a part of the Church but they also feel very strongly about the ways in which they have been hurt in the Church. About this very real and painful problem one hesitates to offer overly facile advice or, worse, dismiss it as something that one will get over. Precisely because the Church can be intimately bound up with the very way one is raised, it is possible to be scarred by the human failures of the Church. At best, one can only say that the Church, in its authentic manifestations, needs to confess its failings. Furthermore, those who have been wounded by the Church still belong within its boundaries since, at the very minimum, they can stand as a prophetic sign about the need for the Church to reform itself. Finally, it is also true, trite as it might sound, that time and good will can heal bitterness.

(5) *The Church has changed so much that I'm not sure I will be comfortable in it.* While it is most certainly true that the Church has undergone a revolution in the past generation, it is also true that there are strong lines of continuity within it. We will discuss those lines of continuity at some length later in this volume. For now, we can offer no greater advice than simply to say·

"Come and see." While a certain "style" of Catholicism has certainly passed from view and, further, it is not certain that one can regain the atmosphere of the old Church, it is likewise true that the Church today is a more open, prayerful, and dynamic Church. If there is one sure thing about the new Church, it is this: there is enough flexibility and freedom within the Church to accommodate the needs of every Catholic and enough challenges and opportunities for everyone to grow into a fuller and more mature Christian.

The examples we have given above are a few of the many reasons why people hesitate at the threshold of the Church. We presume their good will, their first inclination to come back to the communion of those who strive to celebrate Christ in the Church. There are many more things we need to say which we will pursue later in this book. At this juncture let us simply extend a hand in the peace of the Lord and say: Come and see!

II
Faith and the Faith

We would like to begin this chapter with an absolutely crucial distinction. It is one thing to be a person of faith and quite another thing to belong to *the* faith. In other words, one can be a believer without choosing to express that belief by membership in a particular church or denomination. We insist on that distinction precisely because the two quite separate issues are very often confused. People often say that they do not believe "in the Church." What they mean, in reality, is that they have a disagreement with this or that particular aspect of Church teaching or Church practice. That is to get things backward. In the first instance, we should ask if a person is a believer and then inquire into how that stance gets worked out in practice.

In order to clarify that distinction a bit, we will have a few words to say about the nature of belief itself, what it means to believe in God, what we mean by belief in Jesus Christ, and then, finally, how that belief relates to being in the Church. The order we have chosen is not a random one. It is the essential priority of things even if, for many persons, they do not think of things in that order. The plain fact of the matter is, as we noted in the previous chapter, that many people are born into the Church and it is only later in their lives that they confront the question of belief. Such persons are "socialized" as Catholics without ever giving a thought to what it is they actually believe—if they believe at all. We should begin with the notion of faith itself.

FAITH

The word "faith" is a very dense and complex one. We use it in ordinary conversation in phrases such as "I have faith that it will work" or "I have faith in you" with quite different nuances. In the former case we may be simply expressing a wish that something will work while in the latter case we are saying something a bit more emphatic, which is an expression of well founded trust. In either case we use the term "faith" as a counterpoint to the term "know" even if that trust is somehow rooted in an obscure form of knowledge. Faith is not the same as wishful thinking. Faith, then, contains elements of knowledge and trust combined with a certain willingness to commit oneself.

Those elements are also present in religious faith. While it is a matter of Church teaching that persons can come to an unaided and sure knowledge of God's existence by the pure force of human reason, it is not clear that many people arrive at such knowledge through such rational means. Most people affirm God (i.e. have faith in God or believe in God) not because they have strict verifiable evidence but because, in the last analysis, they accept the notion that the world makes sense and that there is some final meaning both to the cosmos and to their own lives. It may be quite difficult for a person to see God clearly in the midst of life but there is, for the believer, a strong conviction that, in the final analysis, everything adds up. That strong conviction is that trust which we call religious faith. When Job cries out "I know that my Redeemer lives" (Job 19:25) his knowledge is the knowledge of faith, not the knowledge of evidence; indeed, everything in Job's life up to that point seems to argue against the reality of God. Nonetheless, Job believes. He is the man of faith.

The crucial point here is that, at its base, religious faith is not merely giving assent to a proposition set out before us but, rather, a basic attitude about the way we live in the world. The usual order of things is to make that basic trust-filled assertion and only after that to try to formulate it into words. Is it not true that many people feel this deep conviction in their lives that they are not alone in the world or that they are watched over and then only after that manage to say "I believe in God."

The practical upshot of that fact is that the true test of whether we believe or not is not to be found in how we assent to this or that doctrine but whether or not we have ultimate trust in the meaningfulness of the world. Theologians like to use the term *fundamental option* to describe that basic orientation by which we say either "yes" or "no" to God who is both the beginning and end of our lives.

At this first, and profoundly basic, level we can say that the religious believer is the one who accepts in faith that there is some ultimate and gracious meaning to life whom we may, either now or in time, name as God. If we can say that we are believers.

BELIEF IN GOD

When we name this ultimate reality we invoke the name of God. The very term "God" can cause people trouble. When some people say, for instance, that they do not believe in God, what they are really saying is that they do not believe in a certain idea of God that they have lodged in their minds or in their imaginations. Paradoxically, the very fact that they reject that notion of God is a healthy sign rather than a symptom of atheism. Who, upon reflection, wants to believe in a God who is simply an authoritarian figure of punishment writ large? Who would invest energies in a sort of super-person known as "The Man Upstairs" or one of those other trivial names by which God gets caricatured?

The issue of what to say about God is a very real one; it is also a problem precisely because we tend to imagine what God is like and we cannot imagine in a void. All of us carry with us a heavy baggage of half forgotten or vivid images which we have absorbed from comic books, catechism class, stained glass windows, popular movies, random sermons, high art, and so on. God can be imagined (and has been imagined) as everyone from a fierce white bearded patriarch to a kindly elderly gentleman who wishes us well.

There is an old joke about a man who tells a friend about having a vision of God. When asked what God was like, he says, "She is black." The shock of the punchline comes from the simple fact that in the imagination we always assume that God is (a) white and (b) male. When we read the Bible closely, however, we soon see that God is described as an absolute mystery who cannot be looked upon, described, or named. God is, and no person has ever seen God. God can come to people either in the majesty of the clouds or through the whispers of light breezes. The basic point of the biblical image of God is that God is not simply us writ large; God is Other.

If it is dangerous to try and imagine God, is it still possible to think of God in such a way that does some justice to divine reality? Perhaps a consideration of the notion of *horizon* might be of some help. If we think of a person's horizon—what he or she can see about life as a whole—we also realize that beyond our experiences, acquaintances, families, etc. there is yet more. Our personal horizon is also framed in the context of a larger horizon. If we keep thinking of that horizon as expanding until we cannot imagine a further horizon, then that which stands behind that final horizon is God. That is why theologians and mystics tell us that we should think of God not simply as someone above us but also as that deep reality which undergirds everything, which stands behind all that we know and love, and in front of everything toward which we aspire. When a theologian like Paul Tillich calls God *the Ground of all being* he is using a term which is borrowed from the mystics: God as Ground; God as the foundational reality of all that is.

What that means in actual practice is that everything that one finds in life, indeed, life itself, exists in a deeper context that is God. When we know, we know in the deeper knowledge of God; when we love, our love is guaranteed by the deep love which is God; our limited existence is anchored in the absolute existence of God.

If we think of God in that fashion we can begin to appreciate what the theologians call the understanding of God which does justice to both divine transcendence and divine immanence. What do those terms mean?

By transcendence we mean simply that God is distinct from and separate from us. We cannot ever quite reach out and touch God; God is beyond us. By immanence we mean that God is close to us, approachable, involved in our lives. To overemphasize divine transcendence is to ultimately think of God as out there beyond the concerns of people. To overemphasize immanence is to make God a projection of our own sentiments and our own needs. The God of the Bible combines both immanence and transcendence.

One of the finest expressions of this balance between God's immanence and transcendence is Martin Buber's formulation (in his classic work *I and Thou*) that God is one who can be "addressed but never expressed." By that expression Buber means that God is a person who can be spoken to and who speaks back (Buber, in fact, calls God the Eternal Thou) but who is beyond our mind's capacity to conceptualize adequately. Every idea we have of God falls short of divine reality.

What that means in practical everyday terms is that God can be found in the midst of life but is never captured or reduced down to mere human experience. The great challenge of the religious believer is to be reflective enough to "see" God in the welter of our hectic life. That requires a willingness to be open to the presence of God in our lives. I have always loved Peter Berger's observation that when a mother wakes up in the night and consoles a restlessly crying child with a phrase like "Now, now, it's all right" she implicitly believes, makes an act of faith in, the solidity and goodness of the universe. In short, we are reassured, we have the capacity to believe and to hope precisely because deep in the mind of the believer there is a profound conviction about the ultimate graciousness of being itself; that graciousness is called God.

One other point needs to be emphasized here. It is that we can never fully exhaust our experience of God. God always remains a deep and profound mystery who draws us but who is never fully known. In that sense we are never believers and people of faith in fact; we are always on the way to belief. When Saint Augustine wrote in the *Confessions* that God has created us for himself and we are restless until we rest in God, he meant that in this life we are always being drawn toward God but until we see "face to face" we remain restless in this life. We note that fact not because we want to be pessimists—precisely the opposite. We want to encourage people to see that the fragility of their faith or its groping quality is not a reason for discouragement. It is, rather, the essential condition of all believers.

JESUS CHRIST

The world has many believers in God who would affirm what we have written above. The language that we use comes, largely but not exclusively, from Christian theologians, but there is nothing in the above paragraph that would be alien, say, to a pious Jew or Muslim. Thus, we now need to raise the following question: How does Jesus of Nazareth, whom Christians call the Christ, fit into this discussion of faith?

This is an enormous question precisely because Jesus the Christ is the center of Christianity in general and Catholicism in particular. The centrality of Jesus brings with it a complexity that we must acknowledge. It is this. When we look at the New Testament account of Jesus in the Gospels, the account(s) of Jesus look straightforward enough. When we further remember, however, that between the accounts of the Gospel and our own time there is a vast chasm of nearly two millennia during which people have wrestled with the meaning of Jesus as he appears in those accounts, the picture becomes infinitely more complex. How do we make sense of all those paintings, sculptures, stained glass windows, treatises, prayers, books, sermons, plays, and personal testimonies that have tried to make sense of this person? Is there any parallel between the Byzantine Christ of majesty and glory and the poor suffering Jesus of Francis of Assisi? Is there any correspondence between the Christ of papal preaching and the last sermon one heard from the lips of some popular television evangelist?

To attempt a mere accounting of the ways in which Jesus has been interpreted in the history of our common culture would require not the rest of this book, but many books. We will not even attempt to sketch out the broad parameters of that question here. We will do something quite a bit more modest. We will satisfy ourselves here with a simple reflection on the way Jesus fits into our broad question of how the person of faith lives out a belief in God from the vantage point of a parallel faith in the person of Jesus.

You will note in the last sentence above that we said "person" and not "doctrine" of Jesus. At the heart of Christian belief is belief in, and faith about, and trust in the person of Jesus Christ. We believe *in* him and not simply things *about* him. What, precisely, do we mean when we say that we believe in Jesus Christ?

First, we affirm that we accept Jesus as the person who tells us most fully what God is like and how we ought to approach God and live in his presence. We accept Jesus as the guide and paradigm of how we ought to live a godly life. We accept, with the most complete trust, that Jesus is the absolute and concrete expression of how we should regard God. When we listen to the words of Christ in the liturgy or meditate on his deeds in the Gospels we have a full and complete confidence that what emerges from his life is the way we should relate to God. When Jesus forgives or calls for mercy or insists that we have an absolute right to call on God for mercy or aid or forgiveness, we can rest assured that that is the way we should relate to God. When Jesus tells us that God will judge us by how we relate to the ''least of the brethren'' we know in faith that that is how God, in fact, regards everyone in life.

It is in the lifelong attempt of believers to try to ''conform'' (the word is Saint Paul's) our lives after the pattern of Christ's life that the believing life of the Christian takes shape. It is in that process of conformation that the relationship between the believer and the Church makes sense. We go to church to worship not because we have already taken on the person of Christ in some definite way but, rather, in order to witness to our desire to do so. We attend the liturgy both to witness to our faith and, in the process, to hear the word in order, yet once again, to deepen our commitment to the person of Jesus and extend it.

Secondly, there is the deeper issue of the death and resurrection of Jesus. Jesus was not simply a great religious teacher (although he was surely that). The faith of the early Christian community rooted itself, not in his teaching, but in the belief that Jesus overcame the power of death and conquered death in his resurrection. Careful scholars of the Bible insist on one point about the early Church: the central issue of their preaching was to witness in their belief that Jesus had been raised from the dead. The New Testament is studded with fragments of early creeds, hymns, and proclamations insisting on this point. One of the most dramatic is Paul's unflinching statement of belief when, under arrest, he stood before the Roman courts of law:

> '' . . . so I stand here testifying both to small and great, saying nothing but what the prophets and Moses said would come to pass: that the Christ must suffer and that, by being the first to rise from

the dead, he would proclaim light both to the people and to the
Gentiles'' (Acts 26:22–23).

There are two things to note about that passage and ones similar
to it. The first is that the resurrection first concerns Jesus and then,
by extension, us. To put it another way: Jesus triumphed over the
power of death and, in that victory, there is hope for the same for
all those who acknowledge that victory.

Death is the ultimate human mystery; it is, as the French philosopher Jean-Paul Sartre once wrote, the shipwreck of existence.
All that we strive for and all that we accomplish both as individuals and members of society or family is framed by the inexora-
bility of death. We emphasize that fact not to be morbid but simply
to note an inescapable datum of our existence. All of us must face
the reality of our death and our deep resistance to the notion of
our own extinction. The resurrection of Jesus is the pledge that
such extinction does not in fact take place. In that sense, our faith
in Jesus is an expression of hope that what, at an ordinary level,
is the tragedy of human existence has been overcome. The mystery of suffering and pain and disappointment (reflected in the
cross of Jesus) is set in the larger frame of triumph over those fearful powers by resurrection. That is why, traditionally, we celebrate Easter in the springtime with lights and flowers and
newness. In that highly charged period of symbolism we say that
the sting of death has been overcome in life.

Resurrection faith should not simply be construed as something
that happens at the end of life or the end of history. A resurrection
faith is one that sees life as a triumph in the midst of daily tragedies
and setbacks. A resurrection faith is one that affirms hope in the
midst of those tragedies where hope seems a slim commodity. It
is by faith in the resurrected Christ that we overcome that most
feared of temptations: the temptation to despair. For the person of
faith the conviction that Christ has overcome the powers of death
is the absolute sign that we are not left to an indifferent, uncaring,

and ultimately chaotic universe. We live in a world that is redeemed and hope-filled.

Thirdly, we need pay attention to the prophetic function of the life of Jesus. To this point we have underscored the person of Jesus as the pledge of hope and the exemplar of how we are to relate to God. When we speak of his prophetic function we mean, not his ability to tell our future, but his capacity to render judgment on our weakness and our failed efforts to live more humanly. The great prophets of the Hebrew Scriptures were persons who spoke with the authority of God. They uttered their ''Thus says the Lord'' as a warning and as a judgment against the people of Israel. The word *prophet* means one who speaks for another, one who comes with authority.

Jesus speaks with this authoritative voice. In that sense, he challenges us in our complacency and strips bare our evasions. When we exalt in our ability to avoid the wrong, Jesus reminds us that we are judged not only by our acts but also by our secret thoughts. When we are pleased with ourselves because we get on with our friends, he reminds us that we must also love our enemies. When we are ready to strike back, he insists that we desist; that we turn the other cheek. When we affirm that we are ready to go the extra mile, he tells us to go two miles. In short, the prophetic person of Jesus tells us that we are not perfect but are called to be perfect.

The Christian person of faith is never ''quite there'' as he or she moves through life. There is always something more: more to give; more to know; more to love; more to forgive. The prophetic character of Jesus reminds us that our life of faith is a process and a pilgrimage that pushes us forward to greater conformity with the person of Jesus himself.

If we insist on the prophetic character of Jesus it is not to make people feel that they are unworthy or failures. Rather, it is to underline the essentially unfinished business of our religious development. It is also a useful way of reminding ourselves that our faith is not superadded to our personalities as a finished product. It is, rather, a challenge and a potency that we enjoy. In the Gospel Jesus tells us to be perfect as God is perfect; he does not say that we are already perfect. In this regard, we are rather like the first apostles and disciples of Jesus: human beings who are attracted in faith to Jesus but still, for all that proximity, weak, argumentative, cowardly, bemused, puzzled, and seekers of divine forgiveness.

THE CHURCH

At this point it should be clear that when we speak of the Church in this chapter on belief we want to insist that one does not believe in the Church the same way that one believes in the God of Jesus Christ. To put it in a positive way: We believe in God and God's presence in Jesus Christ. We believe in those realities as we believe in persons. What we believe about the Church is this: that within the confines of the Church our commitment to the God of Jesus Christ can best be celebrated and deepened.

That point is so important that we need to reiterate it in a few different ways. What we are saying is that the fundamental reason why we are in the Church (or: should remain in the Church) is because we believe (have faith) that it is there that we can best learn about our commitment to God in Jesus Christ. In the order of absolute priorities, then, we affirm a faith in God as God who is revealed in Christ; *then* we affirm that that faith is best articulated in the Church.

If we see that such is the order of priorities, many of the other questions about this or that aspect of the Church fall into proper perspective. The question is not whether one agrees or does not agree with this practice or that doctrine but whether one can affirm one's basic Christian belief in the gracefulness of the universe and the graciousness of the person of Jesus Christ.

Let us leave aside for a moment such questions as whether one must believe in papal primacy or other ecclesiological issues to focus on this much more essential question: Can the Church aid us and sustain us in the development of our Christian faith? Our answer is that it can if we understand what the Church claims itself to be at its most fundamental level: the continuing presence of Jesus in the world through the ministry of preaching the word of God and the celebration of Christ's presence "among us" in its life of worship and sacrament.

If it is possible, for a moment—and this is a difficult thing to do—to forget the Church as we actually experience it either at the level of the local parish or through the depiction of the Church in the media, we might ask ourselves what the Church is as an ideal and what it is essentially. The answer to that question is this: the Church should be seen as the vehicle which bridges the space between the actuality of Jesus Christ in history and us in our own period of history. To say it more simply: the Church is the sign, given by God, that Jesus is still among us both by his word and through his presence in worship. That is it. Everything else—how the Church is organized; how it develops in history; how it further explains itself—is subservient to that simple foundation.

When we see the Church in that light we can rephrase the crucial question of whether or not we ought to be in the Church by asking simply: Does the Church bear witness to Jesus Christ in such a way that I can experience it?

In fairness, we must say that some people answer that question in the negative. They will say (and very often in good faith; not everyone who complains is simply a fault finder) that they come to church precisely to grow in faith and what they get are banal sermons, indifferent liturgies, slovenly sacramental practice, or a host of other less than edifying spectacles of that sort. That happens, and the Church bears a heavy responsibility before God for such a state of affairs.

Yet—and this is the crucial point—one must recognize the human failings of the Church as part and parcel of the Church from its very beginnings. The less than perfect character of the Church is apparent even in the New Testament period as a quick reading of Paul's first letter to the church at Corinth attests. The Church, as I often like to repeat, will be no better or worse than the people who make it up; all of us, as Saint Paul says, have fallen short of the glory of God.

Our willingness to be in the Church, despite the disappointments and the failings that we find there, is a way in which we can affirm that we have faith, not in the Church as an object, but as the place where, through the welter of failure, we can still hear the Gospel and celebrate the presence of Jesus who, in the words of the Gospel, still "dwells among us."

There is another point. Just as we demand that the Church serve as a witness to Jesus the Christ ever more carefully and perfectly, so we also have to take responsibility to see that task is done. We do not join the Church as a lowly private joins the army. We belong to the Church as a believing Christian, as a pilgrim among fellow pilgrims. Seen from that perspective, I am as much a member of the Church as the most exalted hierarch. Thus, we have the privilege of being in the Church but we also have a responsibility.

Our status as a believer also makes us ask ourselves if the Church somehow would be diminished by our absence. Just as the weakness of our faith is strengthened by our presence in the community of believers, so our absence diminishes the pilgrim group who also strives to better the Church by a closer fidelity to Jesus Christ. Saint Paul likes to speak about the building up of the Church. That does not happen in some abstract and ethereal way. It happens when people, in all their imperfection and sinfulness, worship and believe as a community. That communal effort occurs both in the radiant lives of the greatest of saints and among the weakest of the community. It is God who supplies the difference.

The simple conclusion that one can draw from this understanding of the Church is a direct one; it is the theme of this book: Come back. Simply that: Come back. If one feels the need to nourish a sense of God as revealed in Jesus Christ, then one can, in good faith, be in the Church. That is the place to start despite lingering doubts, or an inability to articulate the faith one has with satisfaction, or if there is a lingering sense of hostility or suspicion. It is enough to be open to faith and its deepening.

We insist on this basic approach not to be a minimalist in matters of faith but in order to get priorities in their proper order. The question is not whether one believes in this dogma or that ethical position. It may well be that the believer must confront those issues but only from the position of a prior faith in God in Jesus Christ. It is from there that we begin because, as the disciples said when they were challenged about their own lack of faith by Jesus: ''Where else will we go? You have the words of eternal life.''

It should be clear, now, why we entitled this chapter ''Faith and the Faith.'' By faith we mean that fundamental option for the God of Jesus Christ. By *the* faith, we mean, simply, that complex which we call the Church. Our point is that we are truly members of *the* faith only when we come with that fundamental faith by which we are open to the presence of God in our lives.

III

Worship

Let me go back to our hypothetical troubled student whom we introduced in Chapter I. As part of Mike's explanation for "leaving the Church" is the oft repeated claim that he or she gets nothing out of going to Mass. That statement may or may not be made in bad faith. For some it might be a rationalization but others may genuinely wonder, of a Sunday morning, what is going on up there at the altar and, more to the point, why they are there when they could be on the tennis court or snug in bed. They are, to use that favorite adolescent word, bored.

Although it is a valid point, it would probably do no good (in fact, it does no good; I have tried it) to remind the young critic that before one gets something out of going to church it should be remembered that one goes to church to give something—that one has an obligation to worship.

There is no speedier way to alienate a young person than to raise the idea of obligation. Obligation means rules and rules are there precisely to prick one to ask why they should be obeyed. This is not a reaction peculiar to young people. Few persons are so compliant as to follow rules simply because they are stated. We ask for reasons for rules as if by instinct.

When we speak of obligation, however, we do not have in mind the Church's law that requires attendance at Mass or even the decalogue's injunction that we keep holy the Lord's day. In fact, in this area we are not speaking of rules at all.

Obligation in the sense we are using the term means something akin to an automatic reaction deriving from some cause. If we love someone we are obliged, not by law, but by natural consequence to wish that person well and to express that love. Similarly, if we stand in faith before God we have an obligation to demonstrate that faith in worship not because it is a rule but because worship flows naturally from religious belief.

Ah, as the Bard would say, there's the rub. Our young person feels no obligation to worship not because he is a rule breaker or even because of loss of faith but because the religious faith that is possessed is either very tenuous or even absent. It does no good to hector a person to "get to church" if that person feels no need or urgency to do so. To insist on such attendance is to foster, not faith, but conformity or, what is worse, hypocrisy.

It is precisely because worship flows from faith that we first dealt with faith and now inquire into worship. Note that we are not saying that one must be a person of faith before one can worship. What we are saying is that faith is a priority for the true person of faith. It may well be (and often is) the case that one comes to worship with a less than firm faith. The point is that if that person comes to grow in faith there is already a link between the openness to a deepened sense of belief and the readiness to worship.

Worship is nothing more than making faith concrete. The very fact that people go to church says, as a visible gesture, that they are willing to attest that for that hour they stand before something greater than themselves. Worship is, in its own right, an act of faith.

This gesture is a two way street or, if you prefer the more academic phrase, a dialectical act. By that we mean that just as we make an act of faith by the act of worship, so, conversely, the act of worship strengthens and deepens faith. It is to that dynamic interaction of faith and worship that we wish to attend in the remainder of this chapter.

HEARING THE STORY

It is most instructive to look at the opening verses of the various Gospels. Mark simply announces the beginning of the good news (Gospel) of Jesus Christ, the Son of God. Matthew starts with a family history of Jesus. Luke tells Theophilus that he is ready to embark on an ''orderly account'' of the story of Jesus. John begins with a beautiful poetic hymn in honor of the Word made flesh. After these preliminary remarks each of the writers then begins to tell a story.

We should further recall that the story which they tell is a story that had been remembered by the Church. This is a crucial point. There was first Christ; then his followers; and finally some of those followers committed those stories to paper. The Gospel is a product of the Church and not vice versa. It reflects what the nascent Church community felt about the life, death, and the resurrection of Jesus Christ and their response to it.

Seen in that fashion we are further reminded that the Scriptures do not exist as some kind of free floating *thing* out there beyond community. The Gospel is the product of the faith of the first generation of followers of Jesus who, in the words of Saint Luke, delivered to us this tradition, ''who from the beginning were eye-witnesses and ministers of the word'' (Lk 1:2).

A grasp of that fact helps us to remember that when we go to church for the liturgy we are listening to a story which has been proclaimed in the assembly of believers from the beginning of the Christian Church itself. That is what we mean by the word *tradition;* it is the handing down of this story of Jesus without which there would be no assembly.

There is a further point. Our faith in Jesus comes not from an abstract assent to propositional statements derived from this story (it may happen; it is a rare phenomenon) but because the story we hear rings true to our experience or ''fits'' what we want to know about who we are as human beings. When, for example, Jesus tells the story of the prodigal son we see a way of behaving that, even when we cannot imitate it, we feel is right. We would love to be able to say that those who have wounded us, betrayed us or, in the case of the prodigal son, have wasted our substance can still feel free to come back and we would receive them in love. We may find that hard to do but we know in the deepest recesses of our heart that we would be richer persons for being able to reconcile or love or forgive than to be estranged, hostile, or bitter in our hatred.

Even those stories in the Gospels which seem odd or alien to ways of thinking or our culture can reach across time and intersect with our story if we can just find the key for understanding them. Take, for instance, the many stories of exorcisms—those incidents in which Jesus frees people from demonic powers. The Gospels are so full of such stories that if we tried to cut them out of the story, the whole tenor of the Gospels would be altered.

Our minds are so filled with popular images of demons and so shaped by popular novels and movies that we can miss an important point: to be possessed by demonic powers is to render a person incapable of living like a rational and loving person. They are not in control; something controls them. It is not reductionistic, one could argue, to say that the demonic still lurks in our society. It may be something like enslavement to drugs or it might be something as catastrophic as those poor souls (our prisons and death rows are filled with them) who are so driven by hatred or so twisted by sick fantasies that they reach out to strike or kill or abuse. I would not like to suggest that the power of the exorcist could replace the admittedly difficult work of the therapist but I would insist that the message of the New Testament ministry of Jesus suggests that these demons are not in absolute control and beyond control.

The problem with that above interpretation is that our mind is so filled with popular images that it is difficult to get to the very heart of what Jesus the exorcist was trying to say in his actions.

Jesus the exorcist proclaims that a person's humanity can be healed and that nobody on this earth is fully in the power of evil. In the last analysis, those stories are close to the heart of the message of Jesus: hope and goodness can always triumph over evil.

What we have said about the stories above can be applied equally to the proclamation of the Jesus story as a whole. Those stories are told, not to recall an ancient history, but because in those stories there is always something spoken to us. The reason why the Christmas story generates such response in people is because it deals with a child born into the world under difficult circumstances whose life will arc through tragedy and eventual triumph. We understand the Christmas story precisely because we always look at a newborn child with the hope that the child will live with the happiness we have while avoiding the failures we have experienced. By contrast, the story of the cross seems like a tale of failure and tragedy. It is only when that story is read against the resurrection proclamations that we see how pain, death, and failure are overcome.

RESPONSE TO THE STORY

We have spoken about hearing the story and we have assumed that the hearing takes place in the context of the liturgy; we do not deny that the hearing might take place elsewhere, but the essential character of the Church demands that it proclaim this story as it gathers as Church in its regular worship. We also realize that this proclamation is not always done with conviction or passion or care. There is no need to set out the many complaints about ecclesial deficiencies in this respect.

Our point here is much more modest. It is this: when we hear the word preached and find that it touches our lives we will say, either interiorly or through a formal acclamation, "That is right." Anytime we can say that, we are not only making an act of faith;

we are also uttering a prayer. The first part of the liturgy—the so-called liturgy of the word—is not simply for instruction. The idea is not simply to listen to the readings of the Scriptures and the attendant homily to acquire information. The word is preached in order to provide an opportunity for the person to encounter that word in a deeply personal way. That is the essence of worship. We stand ready to address, and be addressed by, the Eternal Word.

That seems rather grandiose but, on closer examination, it is a truth that should be a great source of encouragement. It means that when we turn to God to listen to God's story in Jesus we may not understand everything; we may be hesitant about some other things; we may feel extremely threatened by still other things. We come to the word with different levels of readiness, understanding, and openness. But, we come. That is the important fact. To come is both an act of faith and the beginnings of prayer. Thus, it is not an exaggeration to say that none of us are fully formed as believers; we are always on the way to belief. As Saint Paul says in his famous image, we see now as in a mirror but, finally, we shall see face to face.

I say that this is a source of encouragement. Why? Because, whether we are returning to church after an absence of years or a faithful member of the Catholic community, we are still on the way to faith. The level of perfection that we possess (and who could ever measure it? who would dare?) is less important than our willingness to be open to God speaking to us. It is precisely that fact that allows the greatest saints to call themselves great sinners without the slightest hint of false modesty while great sinners can still look forward to being great saints.

So what is our response to the story proclaimed by the Church? The Church's response is one word: "Amen." The word *Amen* comes from the Hebrew and means simply "truly" or "it is true." The word is almost always used in the Bible as an affirmation after a hymn of praise. There is a wonderful passage in the Book of

Revelation in which Jesus himself is called Amen: "The words of
the Amen, the faithful and true witness, the beginning of God's
creation" (Rev 3:14).

When we say "Amen" or its functional equivalent to the story
which is proclaimed to us, we are making an act of faith in the
message which we have heard through the story. Our ability to
say "Amen" in short is the taking up of a life of faith. It is the
beginning of our way to Jesus the Christ.

EUCHARIST AS COMMUNION

When we worship we not only hear God's story in conjunction
with our story; we respond to that hearing with our "Amen" of
faith. That, of course, is not all of the Catholic act of worship.
When the readings and prayers with their attendant homily and
recitation of the creed are concluded, gifts of bread and wine are
brought to the altar in order to prepare for the eucharistic celebration.

This part of the liturgy is what Catholics always think of when
they think of the Mass. Anyone who was born in the Church has
a complex memory involving a set of images and experiences
which are at the very heart of the Catholic experience. Who does
not remember the hushed silence during the elevation of the host
with the thin tinkling of the altar bell? Who does not remember
the day of one's First Communion with the mandatory white
clothes, the proud parents, and the high Mass celebrated with all
appropriate pomp and incense? Catholics of a certain age will also
recall the murmured Latin—the "blessed mutter of the Mass"—
and the worn missals of those in the pews.

Those memories, together with remembered (or half-remem-
bered) snatches of the old Baltimore Catechism about the doctrine
of transubstantiation or warnings from teachers about not touching
the host or fears of unworthy Communions because of violations

of the eucharistic fast, have triggered in many Catholics a mixture of fear, awe, nostalgia, and guilt. The Mass seemed so solemn and hieratic. It is that memory which often causes some Catholics to lament the passing of the old Latin Mass.

There is no way in a modest book like this to disentangle the historical or doctrinal or aesthetic components behind these memories. What would be useful would be to sketch out, at a very rudimentary level, a basic attitude toward the central act of worship in our faith.

In order to do this, we might begin with a text from Saint Paul in which he recalls, for the benefit of the Christian community at Corinth, the tradition which he himself had received and then passed on to that community:

> The Lord Jesus on the night when he was betrayed took bread, and when he had given thanks, he broke it and said, "This is my body which is for you. Do this in memory of me." In the same way also the cup, after supper, saying, "This cup is the new covenant in my blood. Do this as often as you drink in memory of me." For as often as you eat this bread and drink the cup, you proclaim the Lord's death until he comes (1 Cor 11:24–26).

I would like to note a number of things in that brief passage which will prove helpful for our discussion. For the sake of simplicity let me quickly list them:

- Communion is set in the context of a celebratory meal. Jesus and his disciples share food.
- The bread and wine stand for the body and blood of Christ and are related in some fashion to his death.
- That death is not the end of the story. This rite is to be done, as Paul explicitly notes, "until he comes."
- The repeated injunction "Do this" indicates that this is not a once and forever event. It is repeatable and is to be repeated.

- There is, in light of the above, some connection between the death of Jesus and our time and the end of time. The event, to use a rather fancy term, is *metahistorical,* which is to say that it overarches history.

What, then, does this highly compressed passage say about us as we attend the liturgy of a Sunday morning?

Let us try to answer this question in the following manner. When we gather around the altar with its gifts of bread and wine we come to share a meal that has a special and sacred character to it. We eat that meal according to a prescribed manner: it is a meal composed of bread and wine; it is eaten while recalling the words of Jesus as they have come down to us from the most ancient traditions of the early Church.

We call this shared meal a Communion which means literally "union with." Union with whom? First, and most obviously, union with the living Christ who will "come again." As Christians we believe that Christ is *sacramentally* (i.e. through signs) present to us in this shared meal. Furthermore, we believe that somehow we participate in the death of Christ and the hope of his coming again as the living Christ who is the end of history.

Secondly, we are in communion with those others who also celebrate those mysteries with us. To put it another way: the Church is never more a Church than when it gathers together to recall, recreate, and re-present the mysteries of Christ in the worship which we call Communion, Eucharist (the word means "thanksgiving"), or the Sacrifice of the Mass. That is the deepest meaning of the terse description of the early Church given in the Acts of the Apostles: "They devoted themselves to the apostles' teachings and fellowship, to the breaking of bread, and the prayers" (Acts 2:42).

To celebrate the liturgy is a preeminent act of faith. It is a concrete and visible sign of the continuing presence of the community of believers in time and space. When we go to the liturgy we join the ranks of believers from the New Testament Church to the present local parish to say, by that very presence, that we affirm our faith not only in Christ but in his continuing real presence among us as a living Lord.

SOME CONCLUSIONS

We have used worship in a narrow but essential fashion to indicate that central act of worship which is the Catholic liturgy. We conceive of that worship as a dual act of listening/responding to God's word in faith and celebrating his presence among us in the Eucharist. Those two acts are joined into a whole. We hear in faith and in that faith are prepared to affirm the reality of Christ in Communion. We come to the liturgy in faith and in order to acquire and strengthen that faith.

It should be obvious that worship in the Catholic tradition is a good deal more inclusive than the celebration of the liturgy. The liturgy is at the core of that worship, but there are also those simple acts of framing the day, morning and evening, in private (or public) prayer. There are those more solemn moments in which we come to church for forgiveness in penance or to seal a child with the waters of baptism or the oils of confirmation. There are those moments when we gather to grieve and pray for our dead or rejoice in the joining of people in matrimony.

Beyond all of those moments for the individual or for the community (such as feast days) is the whole range of devotional and spiritual practices which may or may not appeal to the tastes and temperaments of individuals or cultures. The marvelous (and bewildering) thing about the Church is that, spiritually speaking, there is something for everyone. For those who want an exuberant form of devotion there is the ecstatic style of the charismatics; those who thirst for austerity and solitude can draw from the ascetical or mystical tradition; those whose tastes run to the emotional and vivid can find resources in the devotional tradition.

These divergent traditions all find a home in the Catholic tradition. The very catholicity (i.e. universality) of Catholicity impels us to ask the basic question about the nature of Catholicity itself. If one comes home to, or remains a member of, the Catholic Church, what is one, in fact, committing oneself to? What does "being a Catholic" mean? It is to that issue which we must now turn.

IV

The Catholic Church

What we have discussed in the two previous chapters may seem rather minimalist and somewhat idealized. We have set before the reader a simple proposition: that, at root, faith in the Christian Catholic sense of the term means to take a stand for a gracious God who cares for us and who is best understood and revealed in our celebration of Jesus Christ through listening to the word and sharing in Communion with Christ in the Eucharist.

The reader may object that such a schema does not justify being a member of the Catholic Church. Could not one affirm everything stated above and be a member of another Christian church? Why does such a stance of faith require membership in the Catholic Church?

In the first place, we should affirm, as does the Catholic Church, that one can, in fact, celebrate Jesus Christ outside the confines of the Roman Catholic fold. Even in its narrowest preecumenical days the Roman Catholic Church never denied that there was authentic faith outside of its confines. Since the Second Vatican Council we have come to a deeper understanding of the deep faith of those who stand apart from Rome. Indeed, there is the hope that someday there will be a closer union between the Catholic Church and other Christian churches. Ecumenical discussions have made such a union not an unlikely event.

Our point of departure, however, is to address those who were born or raised in the Catholic tradition and feel themselves, after a period of estrangement, now ready to return to it. Those are the readers who may find what I have said too pat or too schematic. They are the ones who are most likely to say "Yes, but . . . "

The "but" may be followed by their hesitations about their fundamental belief (i.e. they are not quite sure how they believe in God or in Jesus Christ) or by their mixed feelings about the Church and their memories of it. To the first objection, we can only repeat: it is within the Church that faith is nurtured, so if faith is weak, the place to be is in the Church, not apart from it. About the second hesitation we can only suggest that it may be helpful to get a clearer sense of what it means to be a Catholic.

What is a Catholic?

At one level the answer is very simple. A Catholic is a member of that Christian Church which owes its earthly allegiance to the Bishop of Rome, known more familiarly as the Pope. This understanding of Catholicism, unfortunately, carries with it a rather ingrained image of a large corporation with the Pope as an autocratic chairman ordering about a plethora of lieutenants (the bishops), a larger cadre of foremen (the parish priests), and, at the bottom of the corporate structure, the proletarian lay people. This is an image fostered once by the Church and one that lingers today in the minds of many people both inside and outside the Church.

The Second Vatican Council, while hardly denying the hierarchical structure of the Church, was at pains to emphasize another side of the Church. This is a model which emphasizes the Church as a community of people, bonded together by faith and baptism, who are on pilgrimage toward a final destination. In this view of the Church, the image that comes to mind is not a pyramid with the Pope at the apex and the laity at the base line, but a wheel bound together with a balanced center, the holder of the ministry of Peter, the Pope. In either case, there is a recognition of the place of the Pope, but in the latter there is less of a tendency to think of the Church as a monodirectional entity with everyone getting orders from the top. In both cases, likewise, we affirm the authority which derives from the papal office; to think of the papacy as simply being an office of honor would do violence to the Catholic notion of the papacy.

Catholicism is unthinkable apart from the papacy. Still we should emphasize that the papacy carries with it nearly two millennia of history much of which is accidental to the essential office of the Pope as being the sign of the unity of the Church. For now, let us simply try to remind the reader that the papacy is not tiaras, gorgeous processions in the Vatican, blessings from balconies, and the other visuals that are conjured up from the stock footage of the television networks. Those are papal accretions. Nonetheless, the very fact of the historical panoply of the Vatican does forcefully remind us that Catholicism is a tradition. It is that traditional character of Catholicism that bears some closer examination.

TRADITION

Catholicism is preeminently a religion of tradition. It is within the Church that the word of God is handed down (and protected) and the Eucharist is celebrated. It is within the Church, furthermore, that, either consciously or unconsciously, formulations about Jesus in prayer or doctrine or art are remembered and retained. The liturgy is not only the central act of Catholic worship; it is also a repository of Catholic memory. The way we worship, the gestures we make, the clothes the celebrant wears, the order of things, the character of the architecture—all of these things have a history behind them. They echo memories of the past and speak to us of the generations that have recalled and re-presented Jesus Christ in worship.

We make that point about Church tradition not to brag about the Church's antiquity or to praise ancient customs simply because they are ancient. We emphasize tradition because it provides us with an insight into the continuity of the Church while change and innovation takes place. Let us go back to the example of the liturgy to illustrate the point.

If a Catholic who was exiled on a desert island in, say, 1960 were suddenly to come back to civilized life and walk into a contemporary Catholic church, there would be a shock of strangeness and disbelief. He would wonder: "Is this a Catholic church? What has happened to the familiar Latin? Where are all the statues and votive lights that I remember? What are people doing singing? Good Lord! A woman is distributing Communion and another one earlier read the Scriptures. This is not a Catholic church; there has to be a mistake. Maybe some liberal Episcopalians bought the old parish while I was in exile."

Once our exile calmed down and took a second look, he might begin to notice something that he had not seen before. The liturgy still began with the familiar collect prayers and the readings of the Scriptures (albeit in a language he could now understand); there was still a sermon; the offertory, consecration, Lord's Prayer, and Communion were much the same. And, it should be noted, they still took up a collection. So: some things have changed but much has remained the same.

The practical lesson that the exile learned about change and continuity in the liturgy is a microcosm of the change and continuity in the Church as a whole. At the heart of Catholic life is the mystery of God in Jesus Christ. No age fully comprehends and expresses that mystery. Every age must rediscover and relearn how to live in Christ according to the needs and lights of the age. Once that learning takes place, it becomes part of the inherited wisdom of the Church's witness. We look at the great Catholic witnesses of the past as traditional saints or models, but what we must remember is that in their day they were proposing something new and, in many cases, something radical and hitherto untried. Today, Saint Francis of Assisi is safely in our tradition of stained glass and holy card orthodoxy, but in his day his understanding of the Gospel was so revolutionary that it swept Europe like a firestorm.

In a book on the returning Catholic entitled *A Church To Come*

Home To (1982) theologian Mary Durkin and sociologist Andrew Greeley argue convincingly that returning to the Church strongly correlates with the life cycle of a person. We have already made that point at the beginning of this book. A couple with a child may return to the practice of the faith when it is time to send the child off to school. The ostensible reason for that return might be to ''give good example'' to the child, but the deeper if unarticulated reason is often a sense of inserting oneself in a tradition which carries with it values that one wants to affirm and hand on to the next generation.

This sense of tradition also helps to explain why the Church appears to be so conservative. Almost by definition, any institution that puts a high premium on tradition will be conservative. The Church, sensitive to its history and its proclaimed mission as that of conservator of the Gospel, will almost automatically resist change or innovation until it is clear that such a change will not cause a loss of something precious or essential. It is not necessary to agree with the Church on an issue like birth control or abortion to see that its cautious approach to these vexatious questions may not be written off as mere rigidity or obscurantism. Before we make such dismissals out of hand, we should ask: What values is the church trying to conserve? In other words, the better way to understand such issues is not to ask what the church is forbidding but what the church is trying to *conserve.*

The danger, of course, is that the Church can end up by mistaking antiquarianism for tradition. The great challenge of the Church is to hold onto its tradition without ending up as a museum of old, albeit charming, religious practices and attitudes. Many of the raging debates in the contemporary Church (Should only celibate men be ordained to the priesthood? To what degree can local customs be wedded to the liturgy? How should we relate to other churches of the Christian tradition?) are not the result of a breakdown of discipline as some allege but part of the process by which the Church defines its responsibilities to the tradition it has inherited and the needs of contemporary society. These debates, at their best, try to steer a course between reaction and mere trendiness.

SACRAMENTALITY

Sacraments, according to the old catechism definition, are "visible signs, instituted by Christ, that give grace." The Church recognizes seven such signs: baptism, confirmation, penance, Holy Communion, matrimony, holy orders, and anointing of the sick. That understanding of the sacraments is a somewhat narrow one, derived from the Catholic reaction to the Protestant reformers who denied the sacramental status of everything but Holy Communion and baptism.

In this section we would like to propose the idea that there is a wider way of understanding sacraments, and, in that new understanding, we can get a more intimate understanding of Catholicism itself.

We begin with a very ancient notion in the Catholic tradition which is that Christ himself is the first and most authentic sacrament: he is the visible sign given by God to bring God's favor (grace) to us; Jesus Christ is the *magnum sacramentum*—the great sacrament. In this same line, then, the Church itself is also a sacrament: it is the visible sign, instituted by Christ, which continues the salvific work of Christ in time and space. It does this, finally, through its visible signs of the seven sacraments and its manifold presences in the world.

The common thread that runs through the above discussion is that the presence of God among us is available to us through visible signs. This notion of the making visible of God's presence in tactile ways is at the very heart of the Catholic tradition. God's love and concern for us is mediated to us through signs. That fact helps explain the strong *iconic* basis of Catholicism. It is characteristic of the Church that it uses pictures, statues, artistic decoration, etc. It is also a feature of Catholic belief that a person could come to a knowledge, however imperfectly, of God through the works of nature. All of these notions derive from the basic insight that the presence of grace "breaks through" to our life through signs.

This broad understanding of sacramentality (one that was common among the early Fathers and Mothers of the Church) has profound implications for our spiritual development. It means, in the first instance, that we can find the presence of the graciousness of God in all those instances of goodness, graciousness, and love that we find in the midst of ordinary life. We perceive, for example, the meaning of Christian love in the lives of the great saints and in the love that spouses have for each other and for their children. Their lives are a sign-sacrament of God's love for us. The beauty of the world itself is a sign of God's creative care for the universe.

When we grasp that broader sense of sacrament, we can then better appreciate the riches of the Catholic tradition: its art, its prayers, its saints, and its liturgy are all signs of the Church's desire to make present and tactile the graciousness of God in Christ. The seven sacraments can be understood as "peak moments" of this ongoing making present.

The entire concept of the sacraments finds its deepest roots in the mystery of the incarnation. At the heart of Christian belief is the conviction that a person need not seek God. On the contrary, God has made the first gesture: "The Word was made flesh and dwelt among us." That basic fact should help to avoid any temptation to make too sharp a distinction between our workaday life and the life of religion. The fact of the incarnation (and, by extension, the sacramentality implied in that belief) tells us that our world, the world of nature and people, is in God and allowed by the presence of God. It is no wonder that Saint John, in the prologue to his Gospel, echoes the opening verses of the Book of Genesis when he talks about the "Word become flesh." Creation itself is the first great sign of God; the incarnation is the pledge that the created world is still within the gracious care of God's love.

There is a practical lesson to be drawn from this that is so basic that it would seem, at first glance, to be a cliché were it not so profound a truth. It is that the ordinary living out of our life, to the degree that it seeks to be more loving, more just, more concerned—in short, more *human*—is the deepest expression of the Christian life. The Church is interactive with that thirst for full human growth. It is in the Church that we learn to celebrate, sharpen, and develop the following of Christ, but that "Church" behavior is not discontinuous (or: should not be discontinuous) with our life as humans in community.

Let us put it another way. Every time we say grace before meals, receive Communion, honor Mary or the saints, bless our children, confess our failings and sins, or do those other myriad of acts which make up Catholic life, we are, in essence, making visible gestures (i.e. sacramentalizing) our convictions about the reality of God and our determination to plumb the meaning of our lives after the manner of Christ. It is in that textured kind of life where our human story interweaves with the celebratory witness of the Church that the deepest meaning of the sacramental character of Jesus, the visible sign of God's love, is made manifest.

It is that "making concrete" of the presence of Christ that stands beneath the contemporary attempts of the Church to promote social justice. Many people charge the Church with getting into politics when it speaks on the evils of the world condition. In reality, the Church is simply trying to make real the intentions of Jesus who called all of us to be children of God. To strive to be concerned with the poor and dispossessed of the world is to do in our day what Jesus did as a prominent part of his public ministry.

CATHOLICITY

Why do we call the Church the *Catholic* Church? The word "catholic" first meant the Church's general consensus of belief as opposed to heretical or eccentric understandings of the Christian faith. Thus, writers like Saint Augustine distinguished the teaching of the Catholic Church (or the "Great Church") from the dissident sects of Christianity. In time, the word "Catholic" (it comes from the Greek word for "universal") meant both the right and duty of the Church to preach everywhere in the world and its presence in all of the world. After the Reformation, in popular usage, the Catholic Church simply meant the old Western Church with its allegiance to Rome as opposed either to Eastern Orthodoxy or the Reformation churches of the West. What distinguishes the Catholic Church from both Orthodoxy and Protestantism is, as we have noted, that the unity of Catholicism is centered on the Bishop of Rome, the Pope.

What does it mean to belong to the Catholic Church? It means, partially, that we have opted for a certain tradition rather than another one. There is more to it than that. Let us focus our discussion on the idea of the Catholic Church as universal.

To be a member of the universal Church requires a certain level of reflection if it is to be something other than an abstraction. In this regard it is well to recall an aphorism of Rene Dubos about ecology: "Act locally but think globally." That aphorism has direct applicability with respect to being Catholic.

We find our first location as Catholics as members of a worshiping community. In most instances that means a parish or one of the other small worshiping units of the church. That local community is a microcosm of the Church; the patristic writers referred to this community as an *ecclesiola*—the Church in miniature. To be a Catholic, however, means to worship in that local community with an awareness that it is part of a larger community both in time and space. In time we unite our worship with all those who have gone before us as believers. In the liturgy we unite ourselves with the collective memory of all those who have gone before us as believers but who now "sleep the sleep of peace" as the eucharistic prayer says. We are also united in space with all the other *ecclesiolae* who likewise worship locally. While we listen to the proclamation of the word we are asked to recall that the same word is being proclaimed to other bodies who share with us a common faith, a common baptism, and a common Eucharist.

The important point, however, is that while we have a local home in our worshiping community we are not, or, better, should not, be bound to that community in such a fashion that we cannot see beyond it. To be a Catholic is to recall that we are part of the great Church that includes Rome at its hub as well as the poorest mission at the periphery. This sense of joining the universal worship of the Church is both the deepest meaning of being a Catholic and the truest expression of Saint Paul's notion that we are all members of a body that has Christ as its head. In that sense we can think of the Catholic Church as a communion of churches: the common bond of all the worshiping communities who see the Church at Rome as the center of its earthly unity.

With the above in mind, we can make a further point about catholicity: the Church is Catholic by description but it can always become more catholic. By that, we mean not only that the Church should expand numerically and to other places but that it must also expand its understanding of Jesus Christ. That understanding does not come by study alone. It is surely important to reflect on the mysteries of the faith, but it is far more crucial to deepen in a *lived* fashion what it means to be a person who lives in Christ. We become more Catholic, for example, to the degree that we overcome our sense of parochialism in order to live in community with all other believers. We are more Catholic, again, to the degree that we see ways in which the presence of Christ can be made more applicable to the whole arena of life. When the bishops of the United States, to take one example, wrote letters on issues of peace and economic justice, it was not to add their expertise on political and social matters. The purpose of such letters was to reflect as Catholic Christians on matters which are essential to the well-being of all people. The conviction motivating the bishops was to exercise their sense of catholicity: enlarging the Christian vision.

The more we reflect on the notion of catholicity, the more we see its tensions. At times, the American Catholic church has chafed at the regulations "coming from Rome." The papers often reflect on such tensions between papal authority and the autonomy of a particular local church. Without getting into the specifics of such discussions, we can say, at a general level, that such tensions reflect the desire to balance the needs and integrity of the local church with the sense of unity within the whole. The American church can never be absolutely and exclusively American; it must be part of the Great Church if it is to be Catholic. At the same time, it must be free to speak to its condition and express itself in an American manner. The trick is to acquire that delicate equilibrium that permits a church to be local and still an authentic part of the Catholic Church.

In the final analysis, catholicity is the acting out of our common discipleship in Jesus Christ. We are called into communion with Christ as individuals who live in community: the community of the human family; the local community of worship; the bond of all communities in the Great Community of the Church. That discipleship is always on the way to extending itself (sometimes with halting steps) until the Lord comes. That march through history, acting locally but thinking globally, is the essence of what it is to be a Catholic.

V

Living as a Catholic

      To this point in our discussion we have focused our attention on life within the Catholic community as a response in faith expressed in worship. We have further pointed out, parenthetically, that this life of faith ought to have connections with our everyday life. To use the old commonplace: what we profess formally on Sunday should be practiced on Monday.

      Most of us, unless we are cloistered religious, spend a lot of time without explicitly thinking much about our religious life. We do not have the regulated round of daily prayer so typical of monastic life; our surroundings do not provide ready reminders of recalling God. Most of us, in short, do not live in cloisters. Our lives are, typically, lived in the bland world of mass housing, shopping malls, office buildings, and urban rush. The increasingly fewer of us who actually live closer to nature in rural areas are as much influenced by the intrusions of television and video tapes as we are by the slow changes of seasons. The complex cultural signals that we absorb each waking day, while not necessarily anti-Christian, are certainly not explicit reminders of our Christian environment.

      There is a further point. Not long ago the most powerful shaping forces on how we developed our moral outlook on life were limited. When I was a child it was family, church, neighborhood, and the predominant values of my town that gave me my sense of right and wrong. All of those institutions, for example, might tell me that it was wrong to engage in extramarital sex. Privately, I might not have agreed, but *publicly* there was unanimity on that point (despite what people, in fact, may have done in private) from all authoritative quarters. Consider the young person today. He or she might get the same instruction from the same authorities but, and this is the crucial difference, by turning on the television the young person might well see, on the Phil Donahue show, an authority figure (the inevitable clinical psychologist) who will not only disagree with my authority sources but further indicate that they are being benighted about the matter, unscientific, or whatever. Such messages might not countervene what is learned in home and school but it does most emphatically indicate that there are moral choices where once it was thought that there were only moral laws. Furthermore, these moral choices are given weight by being offered by "authorities."

The current demand for standards in school, more parental supervision of children, greater emphasis on ethical instruction, etc. indicates a general feeling that people, especially young people, are overloaded with options and undernourished in their sense of obligation and duty. As a friend of mine said to me recently, "I don't want the school to clarify values for my kids; I want them to tell them that some things are right and some things are wrong. Period."

Catholics might have mixed feelings about my friend's attitude. One of the persistent criticisms of the Church is that it spent too much of its energies thundering out "Thou shall" and "Thou shall not." For many Catholics religion was equated with morality and moralism. That is why so many alienated Catholics, as we have already noted, argue that they can find no home in the Church. They identify the Church with a particular moral position with which they cannot, or will not, agree.

It seems to me that to argue those questions with a person is a doomed strategy precisely because it has the order of things all wrong. One cannot begin with a particular moral issue and argue back to the truth of the Church. What one must do is begin with the absolute fundamentals of the Christian message—the revelation of a gracious God in Jesus Christ—and then ask whether in that acceptance of faith one can make sense of the moral teaching of the Church. That is the insight that undergirds Saint Augustine's powerful and paradoxical dictum: "Love God and do what you please!" In other words, faith flows into action from a kind of inner necessity precisely because authentic faith touches the deepest levels of what it is that makes us truly human. If we can hold on to that notion, the tendency toward reducing faith down to moralism quite readily disappears and, with it, the tendency to look on the Church as a producer of laws rather than a community of those who wish to proclaim Jesus as the Christ.

GRACE AND FORGIVENESS

In his powerful book *The Crucified Jesus Is No Stranger* (1977) Sebastian Moore makes a wonderful, if somewhat startling, observation. Speaking of the various strategies Jesus uses to approach people with his message about the graciousness of God, Moore says that when he speaks to the self-righteous (like some Pharisees) Jesus promotes them to the status of sinners. In Matthew's Gospel (see Mt 5:27ff) he says that to avoid the sin of adultery, forbidden by the commandments, is not enough. He says that to look on women with lust is to commit adultery with them in the heart. The strategy of Jesus was to shatter the self-complacency of the law observers in order to get them to see that, like the common run of humans, they also were sinners.

For others, however, Jesus uses quite a different tack. For the tax collectors who were shunned as traitors and outcasts he showed human solidarity by eating with them—an act that broke the taboos of ritual purity. For the crippled and the possessed and the blind, he offered healing. Since these afflictions were commonly seen as divine curses, the act of Jesus was to say, in effect: I accept you as does God. In the case of both the publicans and the afflicted there was the dual burden of social isolation and self-doubt deriving from a sense of guilt. That the attitude of Jesus was singular is clear from the horrified reactions of those who saw his gestures of fraternity, as when he went to the home of Zacchaeus the rich tax collector: "And when they saw it they all murmured, 'He has gone in to be the guest of a man who is a sinner' " (Lk 19:7).

What we can learn from those incidents in the public ministry of Jesus is a very basic lesson that has application for all of us. It is this: that guilt, the common burden of all people, is not absolute or beyond remedy. Whether a person is shunned by the public acts for which he or she bears responsibility or whether one carries a private burden of remorse, the lesson is the same: God has not abandoned us; indeed, God calls us back to wholeness.

It is in that context that we should understand those opportunities provided in the Church for forgiveness. It is not an accident that the liturgy begins with a confession of sins that expresses our unworthiness before God and others. This penitential rite is a moment to ask for God's forgiveness and to ask reconciliation with the body of worshipers. The implication of that simple confession is to underscore that alienation from God has both personal and social consequences. The fact that all of us make that common confession also underscores that there are no perfect ones in the Church. The confession of sin, whether publicly in the liturgy or privately in the sacrament of penance, is a sign of the Church's deepest conviction about our need to turn (i.e. be converted) back to God who is both the source and finality of our life.

A common perception of grace is that it is a something super-added to us like a spiritual fuel. It would be more precise to think of grace as a relationship. Grace, at base, means simply favor or gift or privilege. When we say "by the grace of God" what we mean is that we have received something out of pure generosity. The self-disclosure of God in creation, in the second creation of the incarnation, in the continuing presence of God in our life, is a never-ending self-giving of God as pure gift to us who are his creatures. That is why the late Karl Rahner loved to say that "all is grace." The gift is not just "out there" as a something; it is bound up with our very existence as humans who are created and redeemed.

When we say, in that loveliest of Catholic prayers, that Mary is "full of grace," what we mean is that in her consent to be the mother of Jesus she has made her life totally available to the end for which God created her. In Mary we find the model for saying with her: "Let it be done to me according to thy word" (see Lk 1:38).

If we can get a full understanding of that dynamic relationship by which God calls us, and we, in our freedom, respond to the call of God, we can go a long way in erasing that simple-minded view that God makes rules and then watches as judge/rewarder to see how we relate to them. It is a thin picture of the Christian life to understand our relationship to God after the fashion of a carrot/stick model of reward and punishment. Our model is something like that which Jesus preached in his parable of the prodigal son. The point of that story is that the relationship between the parent and child was never broken despite the estrangement and neglect of the child. The parent was always there, waiting in patient love, for the return of the prodigal. The father did not say "Pay back what you have squandered" or "Try to make up for what you have done." The father simply "had compassion and ran and embraced him and kissed him" (Lk 15:20). That, in a nutshell, is the relationship of God and God's children.

COMMANDMENTS AND OBLIGATIONS

Lifelong Catholics, having read the above paragraphs, might well say that it is a beautiful set of generalities but the stark reality in the Church is quite different. They might say, bluntly, that their experience has been of a Church that emphasizes rules and point, as evidence, to the ten commandments of the Bible, the laws of the Church, the many instructions from Rome, the directives of local bishops, and the contents of sermons which most decidedly do set out rules to be obeyed or behaviors to be avoided.

That would not be an unfair observation. Nor is it a surprising one. It is one thing to set out a general theory of human behavior; it is quite another thing to make concrete applications in specific instances. As believers we accept that it is wrong to kill. That is part of the moral code of Judaism and Christianity and consistent with everything Jesus stood (and died) for. However, in the concrete instances of living, reality touches law: Is it clear that one cannot kill in self-defense? As a policy of state retribution in matters of justice? In aborting a child to save maternal life? In a just war?

When we go beyond those basic injunctions (after all, no religion or culture urges murder as a positive obligation), the issue becomes even more unclear. Much of Church law, enshrined in such things as the new Code of Canon Law for the entire Church or particular laws for a given nation, reflects the Church's desire for a kind of order that permits the Church to operate in fidelity to its perceived mission. When, for example, the canon law of the Church says that a priest must have permission to exercise his powers to hear confessions (technically called *faculties;* see canon 966), the rule is a safeguard to keep unworthy persons from possibly abusing a Church rite that for many persons is deeply personal. As such, it is a sensible law and its genesis is easy enough to understand.

Between the broad moral imperatives (thou shall not kill) and the narrow ecclesiastical rules (you must have faculties to hear confessions) there is a set of laws/obligations which touch on the ordinary lives of Catholics. It is those laws which can cause a great deal of dissonance for some people. For example, Church law says that Catholics should marry before a priest and two witnesses; it discourages marriages between those of different reli.

gions; it requires a good faith effort on the part of a Catholic who does marry a non-Catholic to raise the children in the faith, etc. Those laws have developed over the centuries as part of the pastoral strategy of the Church to insure the integrity of marriage and the protection of the family.

Whatever the pastoral intentions of the Church, it must be conceded that its marriage legislation, while understandable enough in largely Catholic cultures, has caused considerable problems in areas, like that of North America, where the culture is pluralistic. I have no hard statistics to offer, but my impression is that more Catholics are lost to the Church through mixed marriages than from any other reason. That number increases when one factors in those many people who have had a failed marriage and enter a new one without the blessing of the Church. The problem of mixed marriages and the question of the divorced and remarried is an enormous one. It is issues like those where, at least in the popular estimation, the good will of people can come into negative contact with Church law. This is an enormously complex area both because it has such complicated historical roots and because it touches so intimately on the lives of people.

What can one say about situations like this? Obviously, we could not begin to sort out the complex problems that come from the particular cases that have their roots in human choices and the laws of the Church. There are, however, two general observations that can be made that are applicable to these and similar situations. Let me state them as simply as possible:

(1) The Church is not a perfectionist sect; it is a Church of sinners. Everyone is welcome in the Church (or: should be welcome). The lesson to be derived from that is that if a person wishes to return to the Catholic community, that person should do so. Period. That is the beginning point we assume as a general rule that is applicable for every person of good will.

(2) If there are things in your personal life that make you "irregular" as far as Church law is concerned, then you should seek

out a sympathetic, pastorally minded, priest to help you. They are there; it only takes time to find them. That all priests are institutional time-servers is a canard and a libel. To take the time and put in the effort to find such a priest is not only worthwhile; it is the one necessary thing to do. To find such a priest is a blessing; to have such priests is a great grace for the Church.

To insist that laws serve the person and the community (and not vice versa) is not a statement in favor of anarchy. With the right to be a member of the Catholic community comes corresponding obligations not only to maintain its good order but to cleave closely to the practical working out of the implications of the Gos_ pel. Throughout its history the Church has stood in tension with the predominant culture; indeed, one could argue that when it reflected the culture too closely, it was weakest in its prophetic dimension. One should not expect the Church to mirror all of the values of the culture. When the Church in the United States preaches an unpopular message about the sanctity of human life, the scourge of divorce, the secularism of education, the evils of pornography, or the social inequalities of our society, it irritates large parts of the population. That is not simply because the Church is given over to moralism (although that might happen) but because it has certain basic convictions about who we are and how we should live and what we are ultimately about.

In the practical order the Catholic is bound to listen to the voice of the Church as part of his or her own growth as a Catholic. Conservative Catholics decry a "pick and choose" attitude toward Church teaching while liberals flay the rigidity of those who demand that everyone take the "entire package" or "get out." Such stark choices seem misplaced and misstated. At a basic level, we have an obligation to give the Church a fair hearing in these matters; what might seem to be outdated or old-fashioned ideas might appear, on closer inspection, to be ancient but timely wisdom.

We need to remind ourselves, as the Second Vatican Council taught so clearly, that there is a hierarchy of truths in the Catholic Church. What that means in practice is that a doctrine like the Assumption of Mary only makes sense when one sees it in tandem with more fundamental teachings concerning the nature of the salvific work of Christ. At a more practical level it also means that the full texture of Catholic teaching and practice only makes sense after one makes the fundamental option of belief in Jesus Christ who stands at the heart of the Catholic experience. From that fundamental stance one then ranges out over the totality of the Catholic experience to see how it nourishes and clarifies that first intuition that Jesus is Lord and Savior. That affirmation itself, as Paul remarked, can only be made in the Spirit. What is true in the area of doctrines is also true in the area of morality. We simply cannot look at moral laws as existing as free-floating dictums; they must always be seen in the larger perspective of the Church's view of human nature, human responsibility, and social relationships. Without such a context, moral laws can seem capricious indeed.

Such an approach to the moral law also helps us to understand the relationship of the individual conscience and the teaching of the Church. It has always been fundamental to Catholic belief to insist on the primacy of the conscience; one sins against the truth when one acts against conscience. However, the conscience must be informed, which is to say, educated. In that moral formation the place of the faith is central: Does what I do betray my faith in Jesus the Christ? The conclusion is inescapable: one acts according to conscience but the conscience must be cultivated and developed in the light of the Gospel as it is received in faith and lived in worship.

The relationship between individual conscience and the moral authority of the teaching Church also sheds light on what might be called the ''prophetic'' character of Church teaching. Many of the things that the Church teaches sound hard to many ears. In a country like the United States with its religious pluralism and its tradition of tolerance, the Church's strictures against divorce or abortion might seem sectarian and rigid. Indeed, opinion polls reflect a fair amount of disagreement between what ordinary Catholics think and what official teachers teach.

We all recognize the tensions described above; nor is the Vatican unaware that many good Catholic people simply do not listen to what the Church teaches. At this juncture I would like to propose a suggestion that might seem outrageous to many. It is this: when we most mightily dissent from, or disagree with, some aspect of Church teaching, it is at that moment when we need to be most careful to listen to what the Church is saying.

Why?

The answer is simple. It is of the very character of basic Christian teaching that it challenge and upset our normal understanding of things. That, after all, is what the prophetic nature of the life of Jesus was all about. His message was never a comfort to those secure in their religious or moral positions. He said that love of neighbor took priority over legal observance; he insisted that the despised tax collectors and Samaritans would be first in the kingdom of heaven; he denied that mere formal observance of the ten commandments was good enough; what was deep in the heart was what God looked for.

By analogy we can say the same thing of the Church. It is not the role of the Church to uphold what the majority opinion might be, nor is the role of the Church to ratify what seems most desirable to people. At times, the Church must be prepared to speak truths that are harsh. In the 1980s the American bishops had some very strong things to say about war and peace and economic justice. From some quarters there was a cry of disapproval. Some Catholics even organized formally to combat episcopal thinking on the national economy. That, in itself, is not a bad thing; indeed, the case could be made that it is a desirable thing. The basic point, however, is this: if the bishops as a body speak, we had better listen to what they say before we simply say that they are wrong.

THE INDIVIDUAL AND SOCIETY

The great philosopher Alfred North Whitehead once said that religion was what one did with one's solitariness. It is when, to put it another way, a person stands naked in his or her finitude that the issue of ultimate meaning comes to the fore. It is the balancing of one's own consciousness with the immensity of history and time itself that triggers a response either of faith or of despair. That fact explains why crisis moments often raise the basic questions of belief with such urgency. The great Doctor Johnson put it well when he remarked to Boswell that there is nothing like being sentenced to hang to focus the mind.

That general fact of self-understanding in the face of dramatic existential reality plays a very big part in the experience of Christians. Like the elderly Michelangelo who remarked to a friend that he could still hear the ringing words of Savonarola in his head, I, to this day, remember a hard-bitten Redemptorist parish missionary thundering out the challenge of Jesus: "What does it profit a man if he gain the whole world, if he lose his immortal soul?" Only later did I discover that the Basque soldier Inigo of Loyola used those same words to convert Francis Xavier who later became one of the greatest missionaries of the church. The words of the now forgotten Redemptorist did not make a saintly Jesuit missionary of me but they did burn into the mind of a callow adolescent an important truth: some things are of ultimate importance in the scale of human activities.

This is a lengthy way of getting to my point which is that everyone must eventually come to grips with the stark truth of the claims of faith and respond as an individual. That is what the fundamental option (an idea we have invoked over and over again) is all about. We as individuals must take responsibility for our faith choices.

But, having noted the necessity of that individual choice and the value of that vertical dimension between the person and God, we need make a further point. Christianity is not simply about the individual and God. The vertical dimension of believers standing before God must also be seen in the context of a people who are called as a people. Furthermore, we cannot simply reduce the life of the Christian down to the notion that everything of value happens at the end of life when one is saved.

If there was one thing new about the teaching of the Second Vatican Council, it was in its insistence that faith had a horizontal as well as a vertical dimension; there is, in short, a social dimension to being faithful to Christ. Furthermore, that horizontal dimension does not restrict itself to the society of believers. It means, in the concrete, that we are called upon to build up the earthly city as long as the earthly city is the arena of our life and action.

It is easy to mistake this more horizontal attitude for some kind of political or philosophical attitude. It is not. What it means is that the Catholic cannot be indifferent to the lack of those things which make it impossible for people to live as if they were created in the image and likeness of God. Christians must fight any kind of fatalism which would say that in the end God will take care of people so that their travails are no concern of ours. Even the most cursory reading of the Gospels makes it clear that Jesus spent an inordinate amount of his time doing those things which would make concrete his conviction that everyone is a child of a loving God. Indeed, in the great eschatological sermon which is recorded in the gospel of Saint Matthew (see Mt 25:31ff) Jesus says explicitly that the Judge in the final days will assess each of us using a single criterion: To what capacity were we able to see Christ in the hungry, mournful, thirsty, imprisoned, and afflicted of this world?

How, in the concrete, does one do this? I have no required program to suggest, but the great Catholic apostle to the poor, Peter Maurin (the founder of the Catholic Worker Movement), put it simply and bluntly: Step outside the door of your house and begin doing good!

In the medium sized town where I live (four parishes) lay Catholics are feeding the poor daily at a meal line; sponsoring a shelter for abused children; supporting a program for adoptions and family services; active in organizations to promote peace and to fight abortions and capital punishment; lobbying governments for better and more generous social services, etc. Those efforts are replicated in towns and cities all over the country. They well up from the Christian convictions of people. They are the traditional works of mercy recommended by the Church. They are a living out of the Gospel imperatives of the Beatitudes.

Is that enough? Is it the giving of our excess (money, leisure, etc.) rather than the hard earned and needed widow's pence? It is not my place to judge. It is worthwhile pointing out, however, that acts of generosity trigger further acts. The doing of good for this and that cause may lead us—if we are generous enough—to further efforts or more strenuous activities.

There is a further point. Charity begins at home but, in the Christian scheme of things, it may not stop there. We are, after all, a Catholic, which is to say, universal, church. To act locally does not relieve us of the responsibility to think on a larger and more universal scale: "If one member suffers, all suffer together; if one member is honored, all rejoice together" (1 Cor 12:26).

To cooperate in this Catholic sense of unity, it is not sufficient to slip a dollar into a missioner's collection plate on a given day. The Catholic tradition demands, not just charity, but real responsibility. Our charity is not to be despised; in fact, it is a source of real edification to see the generosity of people in their response to the famines or natural disasters that strike people either at home or abroad. But that admirable generosity does not absolve us from asking deeper and more fundamental questions: Why does the richest nation on earth have so many homeless people? How can farmers go bankrupt from producing so much food that it depresses prices when many people live in subhuman states of starvation? These are not political or economic questions; they are questions that should well up in the mind of every Catholic who hears from the pulpit the words of Jesus about doing it to the least of the brethren.

One of the clear advantages of belonging to a Church which has a worldwide membership and an identifiable head is that we cannot plead ignorance about the needs of those who stand beyond our borders. It would be helpful to imagine the Pope receiving bishops from all over the world bringing to him the range of problems that are merely headlines for us. As a universal pastor he has a duty to call to the attention of one area pressing needs in another. It is not accidental that in the postwar period the Popes have issued a series of letters ranging from Pope John's *Pacem in Terris* to the recent letters of John Paul II calling for world peace, a more equitable arrangement of resources, human rights, and other such questions that touch on the socio-political order. Those papal utterances are not to be construed as editorial comments on the state of the world. They are part of the Church's perceived mission to make incarnate the will of Christ who came, not to save this or that individual, but the world itself.

Not everyone has the possibility or the resources or the temperament to respond to all of these needs. What every Catholic, who desires to be fully Catholic in the sense we have described it, must do is to reach out for ways in which that sense of interdependence can be nurtured. We cannot simply tend our little garden indifferent to the needs and aspirations of the rest of the world. This is not simply a clerical task or one left to the energies of the Church "professionals." It is part of the vocation of every person who gathers around the altar to celebrate the mysteries of faith each Sunday. How one works out the specifics of this vocation is hard to make generalizations about but the need to respond to such a call is rooted in the very act of being a faithful Christian Catholic.

RESOURCES IN THE CHURCH

There are certain things within the Catholic Church which are essential to its identity. In this work we have emphasized the centrality of the exercise of faith in Jesus Christ as it is manifested in the liturgy. It is in that basic gathering of the Church that we hear the word of God and share in the living reality of Christ. It is from that experience that we sustain the convictions of faith which help us to bring Christ to the workaday world.

Over its long history the Church has fostered a vast number of exercises, devotions, and attitudes which overflow from the liturgy or the practice of faith to meet the needs of the many peoples of the Church. It would be well to remember that the Church allows a great variety of spiritualities to respond to the culture, temperament, and aptitudes of these varied persons. Catholic spiritualities range from the austere traditions of mystical and contemplative prayer to the exuberant manifestations of piety so characteristic of the charismatic movement. There are devotions as simple as the rosary and as complex as the monastic offices. There are activist religious orders and those devoted to a life of retirement and solitude.

Besides this range of devotional styles there are certain aspects of the religious life of Catholics which provide us with models for activity. There is the tradition of charity reflected in a figure like Saint Vincent de Paul or the fascination with the religious dimensions of poverty lived out by the early Franciscans and the contemporary Catholic Workers. From the earliest days of the Church men and women have tried to make sense of the relationship between the Gospel and the intellectual currents of the day. Missioners have tried to adapt the Gospel to alien environments; artists have tried to reflect it in the various arts. Heroic men and women of every age have burned out their lives in service to the poor and the marginal and the despised.

It is characteristic of the Catholic tradition that it tries to remember and to learn from these witnesses, past and present. As I have argued in *The Catholic Heritage* (1983) the Catholic tradition does not remember this past solely by enshrining the best achievements in stained glass and marble. The process is far more subtle and dynamic than that. It is a task best described as going back to the authentic sources of the Catholic tradition with an eye on the present. It forces Catholics to ask constantly: What pertinence did a Francis or Teresa of Avila or Newman have for their day which, taking into account historical change, is useful for us? A person like Mother Teresa of Calcutta reflects the perennial task of serving the poor in the name of Christ. Were she transported back in time a millennium she would be doing the same things as she does today. Still, others might find new ministries and new styles for this age which rise up precisely because of some newness in the cultural situation of the times. We have yet to see, for example, a Catholic who has learned to use the electronic media in an authentically creative fashion. The apostle of television (and the computer!) has yet to be born into the Catholic family.

A friend of mine, half in irritation, once said that the Catholic tradition was like a two hundred item salad bar: far too much to put on the plate. My response was that one doesn't try to put everything on the plate; one chooses the right things in order to make a meal. So it is with the Church. The lesson to be learned from the complexity and richness of the Catholic tradition is that there is something there to nourish every temperament and every need. The practical conclusion to be drawn is that one can either find or very easily develop something that can deepen the faith. If one wants a more intense devotional life, there is daily Mass, prayer groups, circles for Bible study, etc. If one feels called to exercise the works of charity one can join the Vincent de Paul Society (or start one, if there is not a local chapter). There are organizations to work for peace, to aid prisoners, to lobby legislators, to do whatever. Most religious orders, convents, and monasteries welcome lay helpers as do missionary groups. For the young (and not so young) there are opportunities to serve the Church for limited periods of time in Catholic equivalents of the Peace Corps.

We should also note that there is a wide variety of tastes in the Catholic Church. North American Catholics might find it silly to dance at Mass but such practices are not only appropriate, but deeply rooted, in African and Amerindian cultures. Similarly, one would not likely find a brass band and fireworks as part of a religious procession in Ireland but such accompaniment is a commonplace in Latin America and Mediterranean countries like Italy. In this area of taste there is, and should be, a wide variety and a generous comprehension of local needs.

A young intellectual once went to a saintly theologian to unburden himself of his religious doubts. After patiently listening, the old man gave a simple piece of advice to the young agnostic: Give alms to the poor. There was much wisdom in that advice. Anyone who wishes to become a mature Catholic could use similar advice. Begin to pray, worship, and start to live out the faith through acts of charity. God will do the rest.

There is a curious dynamic in the *practice* of the faith. One might begin with a certain hesitance or a mechanical routine. In time one gains insight into what is being said and courage in the face of what is being done. The cynic might be inclined to think that one is just becoming habituated to a certain form of behavior; from the perspective of belief, however, one feels, however lightly, the touch of grace. Grace, you will remember, is simply God's favorable estimation and love for us. Being converted is to become aware that that love and favor has always been there.

VI

Coming Back to the Church

This book has been addressed to those who have left the Church for whatever reason and now wish to return to the practice of the faith. It is also addressed to anyone who encourages you in that decision, whether that person be a generous family member or friend or a pastoral worker or priest in the Church. In the final chapter we will say a few words about those who may be coming to the Church for the first time as converts.

We have a basic conviction that we have stated, in one form or another, throughout this modest work. Simply stated, it is that if you are a believer in the God of Jesus Christ or search for belief in that God, you are welcome in the Church. Indeed, the Church is the place for you to be, for the Church is a common pilgrimage of people with varying degrees of intensity of faith who try to discern and live out the will of God. Nobody in the Church is perfect and nobody's imperfection is reason to stay away from the Church.

We should also like to remind the reader of good will that a return to the Church works both ways. It brings a person back into the community of faith and thus helps the person. But such a return also enriches the Church. To put it another way: your absence is noted; as you may need the Church, so the Church also needs you.

To this point, however, we have dealt mainly with general issues of faith and practice and only parenthetically have we made concrete suggestions about the "how" of returning. At this point we might now begin to deal with some practicalities. What will follow may or may not be of value for each and every person's circumstances. There is no way in advance that we can guess what motivates a person to break with the Church and less of a chance that on the pages of this book we could lay out sufficient advice for the person who wishes to return. As a result, even this practical section of "how to" is going to deal in generalities.

I heard one of those electronic preachers once thunder out that God, on Mount Sinai, gave us the ten commandments but some liberal preachers are turning them into the ten suggestions. None of us can claim divinity, so we will not list ten commandments for the returning Catholics, but we will offer ten suggestions. They are not proposed as rigid steps but as signposts which may point in the right direction. Some of these suggestions may be irrelevant for the specific needs that you have. Others may be right on target. I have tried to formulate them in such a way that they could prove useful for the person returning to the Church as well as for the person who is a "practicing" Catholic but desires to deepen the experience of faith.

(1) *Articulate your sense of faith.* Religious faith does not often begin with an intellectual insight that is shaped in the form of a proposition: "Ah, now I believe x or y." More typically a person feels an inchoate sense of moving outside of one's own self-sufficiency because one feels either a larger need or an attraction to go beyond the self. One may be happy and desire Someone to thank or one may be oppressed and bewildered with a strong desire to cry out for help. In either case we could understand those half-understood yearnings as the attractive force of God's presence drawing us back to him.

That is not an uncommon experience. We may be struck forcefully by our love for a child or another person long before we can put it into words. The same thing is true of faith. We may experience a sense of dependence or of longing for "something more" before we can reach out and say what that is.

One way to set out our sense of faith is simply to reflect on what it is that draws us to the practice of faith and what it is that repels or bewilders us. We could make a kind of examination of conscience that focuses, not on our sins, but on our spiritual yearnings: How does my life make sense? What is lacking that faith could fill up? In what ways could Jesus make a difference to me as a person in my concrete situation?

It may come as surprise to think of it this way, but such a sense of scrutiny about the mystery of faith in our lives is already a deep form of prayer. The old penny catechism says that prayer is the "raising of the heart and mind to God." The "heart and mind" is a short-hand way of saying that we turn not only our thoughts to God but also our will toward him. The very act of articulating our desire to be a believer, even if we are unable to declare without hesitation that we are believers, is an act of prayer. We become, in that basic stance, pray-ers.

That final observation requires a word of emphasis. While we frequently set aside formal times for prayer and worship, we should also remember that prayer is, first and foremost, a basic human attitude. It is the mode of being a believer. We are persons of faith precisely because we admit the possibility of prayer.

(2) *Pray for greater faith.* Nobody is a perfect, fully formed believer. The one clear lesson that the history of the saints of the Christian tradition teaches us is that faith must be nourished, deepened, articulated, and strengthened. The New Testament gives clear evidence of this on practically every page. The Gospels can be read as a record of the deficient faith of those who were the closest to Jesus in his public ministry. Rather than pillars of rock, we find fallible men and women who fled at moments of crisis, who, like Peter, would deny Jesus upon close questioning, or who, like Thomas, would demand proof before they would believe. Likewise, Saint Paul, who was called to faith in a dramatic

and shattering manner on the road to Damascus, would repeat his need for greater faith: "Who is weak and I am not weak?" cries out Paul in one of his most impassioned biographical passages (see 2 Cor 11:29).

The great figures of the New Testament were not alone in this desire for greater faith. It is a hallmark of the spiritual search. I have always been struck by Karl Rahner's remark that after a lifetime as a theologian (and his theology sprung from a deep contemplative life of prayer) he had not fully escaped from the temptation to atheism. The reason for this is not hard to find. It has always been an article of Catholic belief that faith, while certain, is obscure. We see, as Paul says in a famous passage, "through a glass darkly." Only in the presence of God do we see "face to face" (see 1 Cor 13:12).

If we are weak in faith, how do we pray for it? The answer is simply to ask. The very fact of prayer is in itself an act of faith. Here is a prayer written by Thomas Merton (it is from his book *Thoughts in Solitude*) that might provide a grounding for the seeker after faith:

> My Lord God, I have no idea where I am going. I do not see the road ahead of me. I cannot know for certain where it will end. Nor do I really know myself, and the fact that I think that I am doing your will does not mean that I am actually doing so. But I believe that the desire to please you actually does please you. And I hope that I have had that desire in all that I am doing. I hope that I will do nothing apart from that desire. And I know that if I do this you will lead me by the right road though I know nothing about it. Therefore will I trust you always though I may seem to be lost and in the shadow of death. I will not fear, for you are ever with me, and you will never leave me to face my perils alone. Amen.

(3) *Attend the liturgy.* The Catholic is a Catholic to the extent that he or she is part of a community. The most fundamental expression of that community is to be found when we gather to-

gether around the altar to listen to God's word and share in the mysteries of the body and blood of the Lord.

One objection that is frequently heard when this advice is offered is that it was precisely going to Mass that alienated the person in the first place. The objector goes on to argue that it was the sloppy sermons, the frequent dunnings for money, the impersonal crowds, the mechanical forms of worship or any number of other things that caused one, either dramatically or little by little, to give up going to Mass on a regular basis.

The objection is not without merit; in other places we have alluded to it. To such persons I have often said (Church authorities will not be pleased with this piece of advice; it counters Church law and diminishes collections!): For a bit forget Sunday Mass and go on a weekday. To find a church which has a weekday Mass where the numbers of people are minimal, where the homily is brief, and the readings done with intelligibility is a great blessing.

The particular merit of attending a weekday Mass (or on many weekdays if circumstances permit) is that it gives one the chance to relearn the experience of attending to the liturgy in a close and intimate fashion. Furthermore, since such attendance is not obligatory it gives one a sense of having done something special and voluntary for God.

(4) *Listen to the word of God.* This piece of advice has a close connection with what we said in (3). In particular, it means that when we attend the liturgy we ought to do it with a renewed sense that what is said in the liturgy should speak to us. We read the Scripture lessons and the prayers but, ideally, they should also read us.

Familiarity does not only breed contempt; it breeds a kind of deafness. We have heard so much so often that we find it hard to truly listen to what is said. It is so easy for us to repeat formulas from the Mass (how often in our life have we said the Lord's Prayer?) or passively take in the words of the Gospel story that they form a kind of background noise.

To combat that familiarity (and all that it brings with it) we need to learn to listen again: "For the word of God is living and active, sharper than any two-edged sword, piercing to the soul and spirit, of joints and marrow, and discerning the thoughts and intentions of the heart" (Heb 4:12; see Eph 6:17).

But how do we learn to listen again? Obviously, we cannot take in every word and phrase from the liturgy. What we can do is to isolate a phrase or a sentiment from the readings or from the liturgical prayers and make that phrase a kind of touchstone for the week (or day) until we attend the liturgy again.

Here is an example of what we mean by such an act. Every time we finish the Lord's Prayer the priest adds a prayer in which he asks that God in his mercy "keep us free from sin and protect us from all anxiety." Why could we not isolate that phrase (or any one like it) and make it our daily prayer until we attend the liturgy again? Each day we could pray: "Lord, keep me from sin and free from all anxiety." The next time we go to Mass we could choose another prayer.

If something from the scriptural readings strikes a particular chord in our heart, we might take a line or phrase or word and use that as a daily prayer. Slowly, but surely, words that are set in a formal setting become words that touch our lives when we are not surrounded by stained glass and sacred art. It is amazing how the once familiar words take on a new resonance when they are said amid the confusion of a busy household or a bustling shopping mall or a high-powered workplace.

(5) *Go back to the sacraments.* This particular suggestion is made with special reference to the reception of the Eucharist in the liturgy.

Again, two common objections spring immediately to mind. Some people say that they are not sure they believe what the Church believes about the real presence or the doctrine of transubstantiation. With greater (or equal) anguish, others may say that they are excluded from the Eucharist because they are not married validly in the Church or because they have been excommunicated or because they wish to continue practicing birth control, etc.

About the first objection, we can only reiterate what we have said in the earlier part of this book: nobody is a perfect believer. In a famous hymn written for the feast of Corpus Christi, Saint Thomas Aquinas calls the Eucharist "food for pilgrims" (*esca viatorum*). That should be a help: the Eucharist is received in faith and, in turn, nourishes. The conclusion to be drawn from this is that we should communicate with as much faith as we can while praying for an increase in faith.

The second objection is far more serious. It admits of no easy solution since there are so many variables. This much can be said There are no insoluble problems. One should go to a reliable priest where those obstacles to full Communion can be overcome either through various Church mechanisms (e.g. marriage tribunals) or through the sacrament of penance. It should be recalled that this sacrament is also called the sacrament of *reconciliation;* that word says something pertinent to this subject. The sacrament of penance, after all, orients itself not only to the forgiveness of sin but to the bringing one back to the community of the believers. It is quite possible that seemingly insoluble problems in terms of Church offices (the so-called external forum) can be solved by a knowledgeable priest in the sacrament of reconciliation (the so-called internal forum).

There is an old principle in Catholic theology: *sacramenta propter homines*—the sacraments exist for the sake of people. On that principle we should pin our hopes. With willingness and faith we should approach the altar of the Lord.

(6) *Act on what you profess.* There are taglines from all over the New Testament that say pithily what we want to say in this section: "By your fruits shall you know them"; "Not everyone who says 'Lord, Lord' will enter the kingdom of heaven"; "What is faith without good works?" etc. The point is simple to the point of being self-evident: one must act on what one professes.

This "acting" operates or, better, should operate at a number of different levels.

First, and most personally, is that faith should change the way in which we live our personal lives. What good does it do if a parent turns back to the practice of the faith if he or she does not amend his or her life, care for the family, or remain faithful to a spouse? This is not a matter of simple moralism; it is a question of honesty. The matter was once put with stark simplicity by Saint John: "If we say we have fellowship with him while we walk in darkness, we lie, and do not live according to the truth" (1 Jn 1:6).

Secondly, we have an obligation to the Catholic community. We cannot simply take passively from that community and give nothing back to it. We are called upon to build up the body of Christ. What that means in the practical sense is that, given our opportunities and capacities, we need to contribute to the many ministries of the Church.

The most heartening thing to emerge from the reforms of the Second Vatican Council has been the explosion of opportunities for laypeople to exercise ministry in the Church. Who would have thought, a generation ago, that there would be a need for lectors, eucharistic ministers, hospital chaplains, permanent married deacons, etc.? Such opportunities are there, and others, some actual and others yet to be imagined, are there waiting for generous souls who understand that the pastoral care of souls is not the exclusive province of the ordained or of church professionals.

Finally, Catholics should be active members of the commonweal. This is not a matter of political activism; it is, rather, a matter of that citizenship which is the responsibility of everyone who lives in community. The peculiar contribution that the Catholic can bring to this task is to judge political decisions in terms of Christian belief and practice. This should not only hold true for those traditional "Catholic" issues (e.g. aid for parochial schools, etc.) but for those questions in which the sense of justice must be fostered: housing for the poor, aid for the elderly, mitigation of violence, etc.

(7) *Christianize your life.* Here we are not talking so much about the amendment of one's moral life as the task of making the practice of the faith, done on a formal level at church, "spill over" into the ordinary living of life.

Such "spillover" can be as simple as introducing grace before meals in the home or the more complex commitment to live in a manner which accords with a Gospel style of life. However one comes to terms with the relationship of formal commitment to Christ in the Church with the informal living style of everyday life, it is clear that if there is not a relationship, faith only operates at the most formal level.

The reverse is also true. To the degree that we can touch our lives with the truths we profess and the Christ we celebrate, we sanctify the world around us. It has been said that the family is the "domestic church." That is another way of saying that the community of the family is a mirror image of the Church in faith and at worship.

It may be a cliché to say that the family that prays together stays together, but like every cliché it contains an irrefutable core of truth. Given the parlous state of the family today and the terrible social consequences that flow from the condition, anything that strengthens the family aids, not only the family itself, but the social fabric as a whole.

(8) *Learn more about your faith.* It may be typical of a professor to insist on learning, but I should hasten to note that my suggestion does not mean that everyone needs to go to divinity school and take a formal course in Catholic theology and advance toward a degree. Nor is it even necessary to "take a course" at all, although this is certainly not a bad idea for those inclined and able to do so.

My suggestion that we learn more about the faith reflects a belief that a modest strategy of becoming an informed Catholic is not only a desirable thing but fundamental for growth in the faith. It never ceases to amaze me that people who are well educated in their area of expertise are often, simultaneously, operating with a grammar school approach to faith. It is at that level that they often run into intellectual difficulties. They reject what they perceive to be Catholic teaching when, in reality, they are rejecting what probably ought to be rejected.

Learning more about the faith involves different kinds of learning ranging from a possession of exact information (does the Church teach what Father X or newspaper Y says it teaches) to that kind of reflective learning which deepens one's understanding of the contents of faith (e.g. Who were the publicans who are mentioned in the Gospels?) to that kind of sapiential learning which affects the very manner in which we live as faithful Catholics (What spiritual writers may nourish my need for prayer?).

Learning more about the faith in particular may range from the habit of reading solid Catholic periodical literature (there is a range of such magazines for every taste and every level of education) in order to ''keep up,'' to a diet of serious spiritual reading and/or theological reflection in order to deepen one's appreciation of the faith.

One of the more conspicuous signs of vitality in the Church after Vatican II has been the veritable explosion of resources for the ordinary Catholic to learn and experience the Church more deeply. Everything from retreats and study days to new printed resources (and tapes and videos) for spiritual and scriptural study proliferate. The expansion of Bible study is a case in point. Rare the parish that does not have a study circle for people who want to learn more about the Scriptures; these study groups have at their disposal inexpensive commentaries, studies, and other texts to unlock the riches of the Scriptures. A friend of mine who is a Jewish scholar of biblical materials (including the Jewish roots of the New Testament) told me recently that Catholics now produce some of the richest biblical materials for lay study in this country.

The thirst for such materials and their widespread use is one of the many hope-filled signs of the contemporary Church.

(9) and (10) *Love the Church/take responsibility for the Church.* I include these two suggestions together because they are mirror images of each other.

For all the blemishes and stains on the Church, it is still, as we have traditionally said, Holy Mother, the Church. It is the historical witness of the reality of Christ in time and space. For every failure of its members, there are innumerable instances of holiness and edification. In every parish we see people who live lives of heroic witness to the truth of the Gospel seated next to the time servers and the hypocrites. For every nun who is mocked in plays and novels, there are unsung heroines who nursed the sick, educated the young, soothed the disturbed, and built the Church in this country. Their story has not been adequately told and perhaps never will be told. For every Pope Alexander VI there is a Francis of Assisi and a Vincent de Paul. For every scandal trumpeted on the pages of the newspapers, there is an unnoticed fidelity of service and love to the poorest and most neglected of the world.

We get some sense of the witness of the Church by paying attention to some of the older churches that dot our cities. To wander around those buildings, built with the sweat and pennies of our immigrant parents and grandparents, is to sense the endless cycles of celebration, the hope expressed at baptisms or at Christmas, the tears of funerals, the joy at First Communions and the pride at confirmations, the silence of so many prayers whispered from the pews or said from the steps of the altar.

To experience that sense of the Church at prayer is not to exercise our capacity for nostalgia alone. Is that not the task of the Church throughout history? Are we immune to the need for celebration and mourning and ecstasy and hope and affirmation? Are we free from the need for silence and penance and thanksgiving? Is our life so complete that we cannot learn from the Scriptures? And, most basically of all, are we so autonomous that we have no impulse toward that Reality which is beneath, above, and in front of us—a Reality whose deepest significance is revealed in Jesus of Nazareth?

The answer, of course, to the above questions is "no." There is nothing unique about us or our age. We are members of the human family with the needs and aspirations that have shaped all other humans; that basic reality is common to all of us. To that basic reality the message of Christ speaks. It is the claim of the Church, an audacious claim to be sure, that it can and does say something "more" to our human experience and in that "more" we fully develop our gift of being "made in the image and likeness of God."

At the same time we cannot be pollyannas about this subject. Were the Church able to fulfill all our aspirations perfectly there would be no need for this little book. People would not leave the Church nor feel estranged from it. But the Church does have its all too evident human side. How do we deal with that?

In the first place, we cannot expect more of the Church than we expect of ourselves as human beings. If we have failings and faults, dark secrets in our heart, and things for which we feel shame, we should not expect it to be otherwise in the Church. While, as Catholics, we believe that the gates of hell will not prevail over the Church and that Christ will be with it until he comes again, it is not less true that the Church is also a field in which wheat and weeds grow side by side.

To acknowledge that fact, however, does not mean that we should sit idly by when things are wrong in the Church; it is not correct to say that "Father (or Bishop) knows best" in every and all circumstances. In fact, as the Second Vatican Council said clearly, the people of the Church have a positive obligation to lend their expertise to the Church as well as an obligation to judge its actions when such judgment seems right.

There is an unresolved tension in the contemporary Church. We still have a hierarchical model of the Church (with the Pope at the top of the triangle and the laity the base) while a more democratizing tendency was set in motion by the events of the last generation of Church life. Let us say it another way, using an older form of language: the Church is a *teaching* Church but it is also a Church that *learns*. That learning process cannot fully take place unless people are willing to express their desires and their needs, their aspirations and their disappointments.

The process by which the Church learns does not always demand a confrontation with accepted practices (although, conceivably, it might), but it surely demands that people should be heard. That, in turn, presupposes that people care enough about the Church to want to say something. It is at that point that love for the Church and criticism of it come together. The greatest enemy of the Church from within is not criticism; it is indifference.

The final book of the Bible, the Book of Revelation, has a very fitting finale. John, the prophetic voice from the island of Patmos, cries out "Come, Lord Jesus!" as if all of his prophecies and visions were goads to make him desire the Lord to come soon. As a Church we wait between the times and in our worship and faith we also await the coming of the Lord. We wait as a people, and as a people we say with the great seer of old: "Come, Lord Jesus! Come!"

VII
A Catholic Invitation

This closing chapter uses the word "catholic" in its title in the etymological sense of "universal." More specifically, it wishes to indicate that while the basic thrust of this little book has been to encourage the person of good will who is so inclined to come back to the Church with joy and trust, it is not limited to those persons. It is also addressed to those Catholics who have never left the Church but who live within it in a very tenuous or underdeveloped manner. It is also directed to those persons who are not Church members but who are attracted to it. Let us say a few words about each of those categories.

Many Catholics, baptized in infancy and raised with a greater or lesser emphasis on Catholic teaching, live in the Church as sometime members. They identify themselves as Catholics and are occasional practitioners of their faith. Others are regular in church attendance but have neither a deep grasp of their faith nor a well grounded spiritual life. The Church means something to them but they are not sure of what that "something" is. In many cases they are living on the energies that they have stored up from their childhood catechism classes. Such Catholics, with encouragement, would love to learn more about their faith (and the "learning" should not be restricted to simple information) in order to deepen their spiritual lives. This is a common enough desire. We all know people, as we have noted before, who are keen professionals in their chosen careers but grade schoolers in their religious education and/or sentiments.

Furthermore, we should remind ourselves that nobody is perfectly formed in the faith or totally mature in the spiritual life.

Catholics do not believe that conversion is a one shot, never to be repeated, experience. Conversion, in the Catholic sense of the term, is that constant turning to God as we accept the grace that God offers us during our life. Hence, besides the returning Catholic and the tenuous Catholic, there is an invitation awaiting every Catholic to "come home." Each one of us can become, like the Church itself, more Catholic.

We also extend an invitation to "come home" to those who have never been members of the Church—the "converts." The number of converts to the Catholic Church in the last twenty years has declined, although there is now a modest upsurge. According to the *Official Catholic Directory* there were 126,000 converts to the Catholic Church in 1965 in the United States. In 1975 that number dropped down to 75,000. In 1985 the number rose to 91,000.

The fluctuating number of converts to the Church has been variously interpreted. Some have seen it as a sure sign of the declining vitality of the Church brought about by the tumults of the post-Vatican II reforms. Others point to the more ecumenical attitude of the Church with its acceptance of the ecclesial reality of other churches. Still others look to the shifting social character of the United States generally. One other explanation can also be found in the less stringent attitude of the Catholic Church toward marriage between Catholics and those who are not Catholic. It may also be that in the period after the Second Vatican Council the Church was so occupied with its own internal reforms that it was less aggressive in preaching the faith to others outside the Church.

Whatever be the reason (all of the above may be part of the answer) it is clear that the Church has an obligation, derived from the Gospel itself, to extend its message to "all the world." The recent emphasis on evangelization in the Church addresses itself not only to revitalization of the household of the Church but to those who would like to join that household. That evangelization effort has been somewhat timid, however, when one compares it to the aggressive energies expended by evangelical and fundamentalist churches to convert people. Catholic efforts, to cite one example, to use the mass media (especially television) in order to evangelize have been, to put it mildly, amateurish, pallid, and uninspired.

One gets the impression that there is a tremendous reservoir of good will toward the Church in the general population but very little in the way of tapping that reservoir. Again, one does not want to generalize, but in my own travels around the country it is a rare thing to see an ad in the newspaper announcing inquiry classes for those interested in the Church or television programs sponsored by Catholics that go much beyond the "talking head" programs featuring clerics talking shop or the televised Mass during the religious ghetto hours of Sunday morning. Or, to see it another way: if one takes the number of converts for 1985 and divides that by the number of active priests, it comes out to about 2.8 converts per priest—not exactly Pentecost Sunday. One of the curious but extremely interesting facts about contemporary Catholicism is that it is in the non-European areas of the world (places like Africa and Indonesia and parts of India) that there is a profound growth of the Church, while we in the West seem to cruise along with a certain complacency. We should also note that in some traditional areas of the world which are very Catholic by tradition (especially in parts of Central America) there has been a very aggressively successful missionary effort launched by fundamentalist Protestants.

EVANGELIZATION

The great mandate of Jesus (see Mt 28:18ff) to his followers is to go out and make "disciples of all nations." That challenge has motivated generations of missionaries to go to the ends of the earth, often under harsh and hostile conditions, to preach the Gospel. In fact, I suspect, our notion of evangelization imagines a priest or nun, in a pith helmet and white robes, preaching to natives and saving pagan babies somewhere far from us. As for this country, evangelization conjures up images of some fanatic on a street corner shouting and passing out gospel tracts to indifferent passersby.

Three observations: (a) evangelization means simply sharing the good news of Jesus Christ under any and all circumstances; (b) this sharing happens in the Church as well as outside of it; (c) it is a positive obligation for every baptized believer. Some may feel the call to be a missionary to a faraway land, while most of us will be content (or constrained) to be missionaries in our own neighborhood. Even for us, the maxim to "act locally but think globally" is valid.

Thinking "locally" means that the most effective instrument for evangelization within the Church is a vibrant parish with a liturgy that is celebrated with fervor and dignity and preaching that is solid and scripturally based. It is one of my deepest convictions that the greatest challenge to the contemporary Church in this country is the development of decent preaching. People dutifully come to church Sunday after Sunday eager to hear something worthwhile. This is an unparalleled opportunity for a parish priest but one that is woefully undervalued and underestimated. Every Sunday a priest has before him a captive (but very willing) audience who are eager and appreciative for something worthwhile to hear. They cry out for bread but, alas, they often receive stones.

To put the matter as bluntly and boldly as possible: the greatest instrument for evangelization within the Church itself is effective, spiritually motivated, theologically nourishing, and adequately presented preaching. It is, of course, one thing to say that and quite another to find such preaching.

Good preaching will occur when two things happen. First, priests must be convinced (and trained) that preaching is an essential part of that ministry and *the* essential instrument of their evangelization efforts. Second, the laity must demand that they get such preaching and, in fairness, make it possible for priests to have the time and setting for effective preaching.

A highly developed sense of the liturgy is crucial (with an emphasis on preaching) because, unlike the "good old days," people today do not attend Mass with the same instinct that they did when there was a strong sense of duty. People not only need to be attracted to church but, again unlike the old days, they will "pick and choose" where they will go. This is a direct offshoot of the change to a vernacular liturgy. In a liturgy where everyone understands the message, simple things like spoken clarity and sensible articulation become paramount. A congregation fed on the professional slickness of television will not tolerate the slovenly celebration of the liturgy or the amateurish and ill prepared sermon of a priest who does not communicate. That is a fact of life which partially explains why (again I cite a 1986 Gallup Poll) seventy-four percent of American Catholics regularly attended Mass in 1958 while only fifty-three percent of Catholics do so now. At no time in the Church's history does the nexus between evangelization and liturgy take on such importance as does our era. The Church ignores that fact at its peril.

What about the evangelization of those who are not members of the Church?

This is a complex question since it involves so many cultural variables. It is much easier to evangelize in a relatively tolerant country such as ours than in a predominantly Moslem country (to cite an extreme example) where missionary activity might be proscribed by law and conversion from Islam to Christianity is a crime. In fact, the issue of missionary activity outside our own country is so complex and so resistant to generalizations that I will leave it aside and speak only about evangelization within the more recognizable context of our own North American culture. About this topic I would like to make three observations.

First, there is the issue of inviting non-practicing Catholics back to the practice of the faith. That form of evangelization forms the background of this present work. It is an activity that occurs in different parts of the Church. In preparation for the 1987 visit of Pope John Paul II to the United States, for example, the dioceses involved began a year of preparation with the invitation to the non-practicing Catholic as a basic motif of the preparations.

Those formal efforts will go on apace. There is good reason for Catholics to add to them by the simple act of inviting friends to go to church with them. It is an obvious but important truth that people will more often respond to the personal invitation of a concerned person when they might be shy about responding to the pleas of a more formal kind. This simple act of personal concern is true evangelization at the grassroots level.

Second, both at the formal level of Church structures and at the same level of informal contact, people who are unchurched should be invited to attend church and/or inquire into the Catholic faith through a course of study. For people who find that a bit intimidating, there is another strategy. People could be invited to share in the good works of the Church through volunteer efforts in works of charity. To ask well-disposed friends to help at a daycare center or at a soupline or to ask them to attend a day of recollection could well be the first step toward exposing them to the riches of the Church's life. That may well be enough; what one sows, another may reap. I have a friend who is a Catholic today because his interest in peacemaking brought him in contact with Pax Christi and, in turn, with the spiritual life of the Church. Another friend is a Catholic because a person once gave her a book by Thomas Merton that he had enjoyed. The possibilities here are endless; it is simply a question of being concerned enough to make a small gesture of sharing.

Finally, there is the issue of those vast numbers of unchurched people who make up a sizable minority of our population. While it is often reported that the vast majority of North Americans believe in God, it is still a fact that many people do not have a Church home. Too often the general public knows the Catholic Church only through lurid accounts of Church disputes or through issues that are peripheral to the essence of the Church; as the old saw has it, the Catholic Church stands in the public mind for "beer, bingo, and birth control."

It would take this book far afield to even begin to sketch out both the obligation to evangelize the unchurched and the methods for doing that effectively. We will content ourselves here with simply noting that it is part of the very essence of the Church to share the treasure of the good news of Jesus Christ. The ways to do that vary; the obligation to do it is simple and straightforward. We should also note that the obligation to evangelize is not only a matter for Church professionals; it is part of the common responsibility of every baptized child of God.

THE CATECHUMENATE

The standard method for receiving a person into the Catholic Church was a very informal one. A person might take a course of instruction from a parish priest either on an individual basis or as part of an "inquirer's class." When the priest and the student were satisfied with the level of instruction, the person was baptized, had his or her confession heard, and began to receive the sacraments. In the case of those who were already baptized, there was a simple profession of faith followed by the reception of the sacraments. Sometimes this process was tied to the liturgical life of the Church. Thus, for instance, a parish might schedule the inquiry class in such a way that it finished toward the end of the Lenten season so that the members of the class could be received into the church at the Easter Vigil service when baptisms make up an integral part of the service.

In 1972 the Vatican's Congregation for Divine Worship (the Church office that oversees Catholic liturgy) issued guidelines for the institution of the "Rite of Christian Initiation of Adults" (RCIA). In effect, the Vatican (at the request of many bishops from around the world) reinstituted an ancient usage, characteristic of the early Church, which was called the catechumenate.

The word "catechumen" like the word "catechism" comes from the Greek verb *katechein,* "to teach." The catechumens of the early Church were those who wished to join the Church and who had formally enrolled in a class in order to receive instruction and to go through the various ceremonies leading up to baptism. The length of the catechumenate could vary from a year to four years. Eventually, as adult converts lessened in number through the slow Christianization of Europe, the catechumenate disappeared in the Church. Its memory was retained in the ceremonies that were part of the baptismal rite for infants and adults. Those ceremonies (the profession of faith; the anointings, etc.) were a telescoped version of rites which, originally, were spread out over a period of the liturgical year.

When the Vatican, in 1972, reinstituted the catechumenate, its aim was to integrate the process of becoming a Catholic Christian into the worship life of the Church. Rather than having the potential convert acquire information (through the inquiry class) and then proceed to the sacraments, RCIA intends to initiate the person into the life of worship through a graduated process of worship and teaching done in the context of the liturgy. This intention was stated clearly in the introduction to the 1972 instruction issued by the Congregation for Divine Worship: "They [i.e. the adult catechumens] hear the preaching of the mystery of Christ, The Holy Spirit opens their hearts, and they freely and knowingly seek the living God and enter the path of faith and conversion. By God's help, they will be strengthened spiritually in their preparation and at the proper time they will receive the sacraments fruitfully" (*The Rites of the Catholic Church,* New York: Pueblo, 1976, p. 20).

We can consider RCIA as a process that may vary in length according to the needs and exigencies of the local congregation.

That process has various stages which we can briefly describe as being:

(1) The period of initial inquiry in which people make known their intention to join the believing community.

(2) The catechumenate. This period is begun with appropriate liturgical rites which signifies that the person is now an actual member of the Church as he or she begins a period of learning and a time of practicing the faith.

(3) The period of enlightenment. This time of preparation for the reception of the sacraments is a period of intense spiritual preparation leading up to the sacraments of initiation (baptism, penance, confirmation, the reception of the Eucharist). Ideally, this time of enlightenment should coincide with the Lenten season which is the general preparation for the celebration of Easter.

(4) Reception of the sacraments. This is the apex of the RCIA experience. It is most appropriately celebrated at the Easter Vigil which is the traditional time for such ceremonies.

(5) Post-initiation growth. After the full liturgical reception into the worshiping life of the Church, there is, ideally, some kind of "follow-up" program to incorporate the person into the full community of the congregation's life. The precise character of this program will vary from parish to parish.

The RCIA process is not obligatory in American parishes yet and its use depends a great deal on the energies and needs of the local parish. One of the parishes in my hometown serves a huge student population from the neighboring university. RCIA has been impossible to initiate there because students are not permanent members of the parish and few of them remain in the city over Easter which would be the ideal time to culminate the RCIA experience. Hence, the chaplain has had to find his own methods for dealing with the students who wish to join the Church.

Whatever practical difficulties may be encountered with the implementation of RCIA, there is no gainsaying the fact that its fundamental intuition is on target: to understand the process of becoming a Christian as a *religious and Christian* process by which one becomes active in the believing community. And that is the precise motive that energizes the RCIA program. For that reason we should also note that the program may also be appropriate for the "returning Catholic." Even though a person is baptized, his or her connection with the faith may be so slim that RCIA might well be a way of relearning and re-experiencing growth in the faith in a structured and spiritual manner. The only difference between the returning Catholic and the convert would be the number of the sacraments of initiation to be received at the Easter Vigil. Those baptized and confirmed, of course, do not receive these sacraments again.

FAITH: A SUMMARY STATEMENT

The capacity to believe is not something that one can work for; one receives it as a gift but, having received it, faith can be nurtured into greater growth and maturity. We believe that anyone who desires to come back to the practice of religion or who feels a call to seek out the Church is, in effect, receiving an invitation to belief from God. It is the work of grace. Faith, as it were, engenders greater faith. Cooperation with grace brings with it the promise of greater grace. It is one of the curious facts about many of the greatest Christians that they were already people of faith when, under the impulse of God's grace, they were able to take another great stride on the Christian journey. Mother Teresa, for example, had been an exemplary nun for some years when, as she has said, she looked out of a train window and, for the first time, really *saw* the poor teeming masses of India. It was that second conversion experience that led her to leave her convent and begin to work directly with the dying destitute of Calcutta.

Few of us receive the extraordinary call of a Mother Teresa;

few of us, I suspect, would even want such a call. All of us, however, are called, first to faith, and then to greater faith.

How is faith nurtured? First, let us insist that it must be nurtured. We do grow in faith. And, further, this growth in faith is always an open-ended affair. Our faith is never perfect; it never peaks or reaches a plateau.

Faith is first nurtured by *listening:* "So faith comes from what is heard and what is heard comes by the preaching of Christ" (Rom 10:17). This "hearing" and "listening" means not only the formal hearing of the sermon or readings of the Scriptures (although it surely means that also) but also listening to the quiet promptings of the heart in the silence of prayer or the urgings of the heart during the celebration of the Eucharist. In fact, we can say that listening and hearing can be reduced down to that basic readiness to be open to the voice of God in any and all circumstances. At this level, faith and prayer are intermixed. We pray for faith, and in faith we pray. In both instances there is that fundamental openness to the awe-ful mystery which is God and that profound humanity which is the revelation of Jesus as the Christ.

Faith is then strengthened by *doing.* The matter is put succinctly by Saint James: "But be doers of the word and not hearers only" (Jas 1:22). This, of course, is only a variation on the Gospel observation that by "their fruits shall you know them." It is also an application of the common-sense observation of everyone who argues that if a person professes a religious faith it should somehow translate into action.

At a personal level we know this to be true. In fact, one reason why people hesitate to embrace the life of faith is because they recognize that they should change as a result of their commitment toward the life of faith. Saint Augustine in *The Confessions* makes the point very succinctly. As he edged toward faith Augustine knew that he would have to leave off his dissolute life; thus, he prayed, "Lord, make me chaste but not just yet."

This "doing" of the faith does not mean a simple change in

one's personal habits. Doing cannot be equated with personal morality. Doing also includes the active life of living with a sense of justice and love, with a sense of compassion and duty, with a willingness to give rather than to receive. It means, in short, a conversion of life. This conversion involves not only the way we look at things but the way we act. That intimate connection between hearing and doing has been so perfectly summed up by Saint John in the New Testament that we will let it stand as the coda of this chapter and this book:

> Beloved let us love one another; for love is of God, and he who loves is born of love and knows God. He who does not love does not know God; for God is love. In this the love of God was made manifest among us, that God sent his only Son into the world so that we might live through him. In this is love, not that we loved God but that he loved us and sent his Son to be an expiation for our sins. Beloved, if God so loved us, we also ought to love one another. No man has ever seen God; if we love one another, God abides in us and his love is perfected in us (1 Jn 4:7–12).

Appendix: Some Basic Readings

This book has been kept free of footnotes; at a very few places we have mentioned books in the text itself. This appendix will serve two functions: (a) to give the interested reader some sense of where the author got his information; (b) to provide some hints as to where one might go to read in greater depth about the matters dealt with in this book.

While there is a fair amount of journalistic reporting about people who leave the Church and/or return, the subject has received relatively little serious book length treatment. Mary Durkin and Andrew Greeley's *A Church To Come Home To* (Chicago: Thomas More, 1982) addresses itself explicitly to the returning Catholic. Dean Hoge, the sociologist at Catholic University, has published a survey of the problem: *Converts, Dropouts, and Returnees: A Study of Religious Change among Catholics* (New York: Pilgrim, 1981). William Willimon's *What's Right with the Church* (San Francisco: Harper and Row, 1985) is a well-written defense of Church membership written from a Protestant perspective.

A good deal of the material in this book draws on three earlier works of mine: *The Catholic Heritage* (New York: Crossroad, 1983); *The Catholic Experience* (New York: Crossroad, 1985); *The Catholic Faith: An Introduction* (Mahwah: Paulist, 1987). There are any number of other fine introductions to Catholic belief and practice. The most comprehensive is Richard McBrien's two-volume work *Catholicism* (Minneapolis: Winston, 1981) which is also available in a one-volume study edition. John and Denise Carmody's *Contemporary Catholic Theology: An Introduction* (San Francisco: Harper and Row, 1980; rev. ed. 1985) is a readable work done in the Rahnerian mode. Monika Hellwig's *Understanding Catholicism* (Mahwah: Paulist, 1980) combines theology and spirituality in a compelling manner. Matthew Kohmescher's *Catholicism Today* (Mahwah: Paulist, 1980) is a very brief survey of Catholic belief and practice.

Books which deal with specific topics in Catholicism come off the press without end. Some recent volumes of interest are pertinent to our needs. Bernard Cooke's *Sacraments and Sacramentality* (Mystic: Twenty-Third Publications, 1984) is a splendid and readable introduction to the sacramental life of the church. Berard Marthaler's *The Creed* (Mystic: Twenty-Third Publications, 1987) is a comprehensive meditation on the articles of the Apostles' Creed. Stephen Happel and David Tracy's *A Catholic Vision* (Philadelphia: Fortress, 1984) is a brief but lively history of the Catholic tradition. Women have recently begun to find their voice in the Catholic Church. Mary Jo Weaver's *New Catholic Women* (San Francisco: Harper and Row, 1986) is an excellent overview, both historical and doctrinal, of women in the Catholic tradition with a special emphasis on contemporary issues.

For the intellectually adventuresome, Karl Rahner's *Foundations of Christian Faith* (New York: Seabury, 1978) would be the book to read. It is the summary of Rahner's long meditation on belief in the modern world. Rahner is a difficult writer, so we are in debt to Leo O'Donovan for editing *A World of Grace* (New York: Crossroad, 1980) which has essays by eminent Rahnerians keyed to the text of *Foundation*.

Those interested in spirituality have a wealth of primary material these days to choose from. A handy little book with practical hints for the life of prayer is David Hassel's *Radical Prayer* (Mahwah: Paulist, 1983). For an extremely readable introduction to contemplative prayer using the method of "centering"

Thomas Keating's *Open Heart, Open Mind* (Warwick: Amity House, 1986) is both simple and profound. Kevin Irwin's *Liturgy, Prayer, and Spirituality* (Mahwah: Paulist, 1984) is a fine treatment of prayer from the perspective of the liturgy. Gertrud Mueller Nelson's *To Dance with God* (Mahwah: Paulist, 1986) is a handy compendium of suggestions for family devotions and rituals. The Rite of Christian Initiation of Adults (RCIA) is still in a state of flux in the American church but there is useful information on the program and its rites in Gary Timmons' *Welcome: An Adult Education Program Based on RCIA* (Mahwah: Paulist, 1982) and Rosalie Curtin *et al.*, *RCIA: A Practical Approach to Christian Initiation for Adults* (Dubuque: William Brown, 1981). Finally, while there are numerous resources for learning about the spirituality of the Catholic Church such as the many volumes of primary sources in the Paulist series entitled *The Classics of Western Spirituality*, one handy volume which surveys the field of spirituality can be highly recommended: *The Study of Spirituality*, edited by Cheslyn Jones, Geoffrey Wainwright, and Edward Yarnold (New York: Oxford University Press, 1986).

At the core of the Catholic's reading should be the writings of Sacred Scripture. There are so many good translations available today that one hesitates to recommend one over another. The best strategy might be to find the one that reads best for you. Most of the biblical quotes in this volume, for example, are from the Revised Standard Version (Protestant) because I like the prose renderings; the New American Bible and the Jerusalem Bible are both excellent Catholic translations. Some people like to read the old King James Version simply because of the majesty of the language. The one caveat I would offer, however, is to avoid paraphrases like the now popular *The Book* and *The Living Bible* both because they are paraphrases and, what is worse, paraphrases with a decided doctrinal slant. Lawrence Boadt's *Reading the Old Testament: An Introduction*

(Mahwah: Paulist, 1984) is a handy and inexpensive aid for the reading of the Hebrew Scriptures. Raymond Collins' *Introduction to the New Testament* (Garden City: Doubleday, 1982), is an excellent Catholic introduction to the New Testament; both volumes have suggestions for further reading.